PLYMOUTH
More
PICTURES FROM THE PAST

Guy Fleming

DEVON BOOKS

First published in Great Britain in 1996 by Devon Books

British Library Cataloguing-in-Publication Data
A CIP Catalogue Record for this book is available from the British Library

ISBN 0 86114 903 3

DEVON BOOKS
Official Publisher to Devon County Council

Halsgrove House
Lower Moor Way
Tiverton, Devon EX16 6SS

Telephone: 01884 243242
Facsimile: 01884 243325

Printed and bound in Great Britain by
The Devonshire Press Ltd, Torquay

~ CONTENTS ~

~ *INTRODUCTION* ~

When Guy Fleming first decided to take his weekly trip down memory lane in the *Evening Herald's* Pictures From The Past we knew readers would be keen to follow him.

What we didn't anticipate was the overwhelming response of photographs and recollections which fed the column for so many years and has now helped to bring about a second book.

Plymothians have amused us and amazed us with their insights into days gone by and I am sure this latest compendium will continue the tradition.

Keith Scrivener
Deputy Editor
Evening Herald
June 1996

~ ACKNOWLEDGEMENTS ~

The author and publisher are grateful to all the individuals who provided information and photographs that were used in the original newspaper features for the *Evening Herald*, and without whom this book could not have been produced.

Thanks also to Deborah Martin who edited the original newspaper articles for use in this book, and to the *Western Morning News* for their help in providing photographs from their archives.

Wayne Perry, Evening Herald

The Author.

GENTLEMEN TRAM DRIVERS
OF DAYS GONE BY

Photographs of trams always bring back memories and this one, taken in 1938, reminded several Evening Herald readers of days long since passed.

Mr F.G. Frampton pointed out that the particular tram shown, No. 158, was the last one to run on the final route from Peverell to Old Town Street, in 1945. Well might he know – he was a conductor on that tram during the 1940s and the picture brought back happy memories. The fares, he said, ranged from one-and-a-half to four old pence.

He remembered particularly three 'gentlemen drivers' – Dick Gluyas, Bert Herring and George White. He recalled: 'There were no meal breaks but my driver's son, Peter Gluyas, used to bring us a can of tea. I warmed my pasties on a heater on the tram platform.'

Another reader remembered that the tram ran for the last time at 5.30 p.m. on 29 September 1945. Later, she said, it was taken to Home Park (the football ground) where, with other old trams, it was used as the director's stand. How times have changed!

Mrs J. Curle remembered catching the tram to visit her grandmother in Peverell. 'I loved sitting on the top, swaying from side to side as we trundled along the rails. The seats were wooden and not very comfortable, but the drivers were always friendly and helpful. There was a "driving" handle at each end of the tram with an overhead electrified arm to run along the electric cable to power it. When the tram reached its terminus the driver would get down and pull a rope to change its position for the return journey. He would use the handle at the other end to control it.'

Mr T. Taylor identified the location of the picture as Mutley Plain in summer – indicated by the light clothing the people are wearing – and

A nostalgic sight – one of Plymouth's last trams

pointed out that the little open car, parked in the wrong direction, would certainly cause chaos today.

Mrs J.M. Hassall noticed the tower of the now-demolished Methodist Church, visible above the vehicle. She also observed that only two of the trees shown in the picture still survive.

DEVONPORT AND PLYMPTON IN THE EARLY YEARS OF THE CENTURY

Many people recognised this photograph of Plympton, taken about eighty years ago. Mr C. Nicholls, now in his eighties, identified the buildings that can be seen: (from the bottom upwards) the Old Priory, St Mary's Church, Boringdon Villas, Alston House and Treverbyn House.

Ridgeway, Plympton, in the 1920s.

Fore Street, Devonport, in 1904.

Of course, the whole scene has long since been covered by suburbia, much of it erected in the 1930s.

The lower photograph shows Fore Street, Devonport in 1904. Among the buildings identified by readers are the Two Trees pub, the Evening Herald office, Bateman's the opticians, Tozers the drapers and the Royal Hotel, all on the right.

May's the grocer and Oliver's the boot and shoe shop are prominent on the left.

~ A GIANT OF A MAN ~

Some described him as 'a great Devonport man'; others said he was a larger-than-life figure. But all agreed that twenty-stone 'Putty' Philpotts, seen here striding across Plymouth Hoe in his Longjohns and costume, was a real character. Ex-Navy, and later a publican, he is pictured heading the combined Plymouth, Stonehouse and Devonport carnival procession in 1926.

The carnival lasted a week and was a fun-filled annual event before the war. It attracted huge crowds and raised money for the much-loved Royal Albert Hospital, as Devonport Hospital used to be known. Thousands of poeple always watched the procession – there was no fear of mugging in those days.

On seeing the photo, Putty's grandson, Mr Colin Whiting, wrote in with details about his grandfather. He revealed that Putty had been the heaviest

Putty Philpotts leading the carnival procession in 1926.

Lily Pocock dressed for the carnival.

man in the Royal Navy, and a painter by trade. After he left the Service he became mine host at the Brunswick Hotel in High Street, Stonehouse. There, it seems, 'he entertained his clientele by playing his banjo sitting by the log fire in the public bar. Stars from the Palace Theatre used to visit, joining in many a singsong. Putty's favourite past-time was writing lyrics to existing songs, such as "South of the Border". This became "South of the Border down Stonehouse Bridge Way", with about ten verses.'

Mr Whiting added that when the Brunswick was destroyed by a land mine during the war, Putty Philpotts took over the tenancy of a pub in Devonport, only to be bombed out again – and on his very first night! He finally took over No-Place Inn, Eldad Hill, where he ended his days.

Another reader remembered that Putty went to the Gunnislake area in between these tenancies and that he starred in several concerts. One of his songs was 'Figgy Pudding'.

Enid Ware recalled the fun of Plymouth's pre-war carnival weeks. There were parades every day, she said. 'When we came from school at four o'clock, we got into fancy-dress and joined in the fun. Plymouth was so alive and friendly then. Mr Philpotts was such a jolly character and so right for carnival king.'

Mr Whiting identified the carnival queen in this picture as Edith Mayne, while another reader, Mrs Vera Flood, remembered the carnival and said that she had a photo of it taken outside Devonport Hospital. It showed the carnival king and queen with their retinue and hospital staff, 'including myself – I was staff nurse'.

Other reminiscences of Putty Philpott included one from J. Sommers who suggested that Putty had been a one-time doorman at the Palace Theatre. E.F. Higgins, meanwhile, recalled that when Putty died his funeral bearers 'had to be fortified at the local bar before carrying out their bulky task!'

Where are such characters to be found in the life of Plymouth today?

~ SERVING TEA FOR THE GUESTS ~

'Tea for two, ma'am? Why, certainly – at once.' The butler bows slightly and nudges the waiting maid into the house, away from the guests dropped by the front lawns of the smart, detached houses in Molesworth Road.

The spotlessly attired grooms jump into their well-liveried carriages, crack their whips and the horses obediently canter off up the hill towards the small village of Stoke.

It all happened just like that, before the turn of the century, Miss Joan Stivey reported. One of the houses shown in this picture of Molesworth Road was her family home; it was no. 5, part of the way up on the left-hand side, with a cart seen passing it. Miss Stivey pointed out that the picture was taken from the Millbridge crossroads.

'The house was bought by my great-grandparents. My father was born

Molesworth Road seen from Millbridge cross-roads.

there in 1887 and died there in 1971, having lived most of his life in the house. Maybe the photo shows his mother or his aunt!'

Miss Stivey's grandmother told her about the social life enjoyed by the occupants of Mount Edgcumbe Terrace opposite, somewhat hidden by the tall trees. 'Doctors, lawyers, naval and army officers lived there,' she explained. Her grandmother remembered summer afternoons when tea was served on the front lawns of those imposing houses, 'with butlers and parlour maids waiting on their employers'.

'The large wrought-iron gates kept the "ordinary folk" out of the drive; now only the stone pillars are left,' she added.

Local writer Joy David also has a personal involvement with the photo because her grandfather, William George, and his wife, ran the cash draper's with his name on the awning. They lived opposite in Valletort House. 'Subsequently, he moved to Mount Edgcumbe Terrace. He had by this time purchased the Lidstone Billing Company, which still exists today.'

Mrs Marie Pearn bought a hat at the shop when she was ten, and her parents kept a shop a little further down. 'The end shop was Viggers Dairy and the chemist's was owned by Mr Davies,' she recalled. 'Body, the iron-mongers, and the post office were further down the road. Chedd the tobacconists, Rescorla fruiterers, Prowse bakers, Harris meat and fish and chip shop, Eastman the butchers and Charles the tailors were also there, near the lovely Victoria Park.

'There was a toll gate at the bottom of Millbridge where Jones, the ice cream man, sold glasses of ice cream for 1s. 2d.'

~ *A RED FLAG IN ST BUDEAUX* ~

Is there a doctor in the house? Years ago in St Budeaux the red flag would tell you, for the local family doctor, Dr A.C.F. Smith, ran up a flag on the pole in his garden to let it be known he was on his rounds and unavailable at home.

Local historian Marshall Ware provided this intriguing piece of information in response to the picture of the old village taken from the former Barne Barton Farm, looking towards the Square. He pointed out that the large house seen in the picture, Meera, was built in 1903 by Dr Smith and his wife, the Hon. Esther Eleanor Smith, at a cost of £1000.

As for the horse and cart seen on the railway bridge, Mr Ware thought it was Mr Cuddeford's milk float. Directly ahead is the Trelawny Hotel, built in 1895. Mr Ware remembered that the shop in Yeoman's Terrace was Tom Occleshaw's hairdressing and tobacconist's, then lit by oil lamps.

The open land in the distance contained the local horse show and football club fields. 'Mr Bradford cultivated the fields which produced good root crops, carrots, turnips, etc., resulting from organic farming and crop rotation. He held the contract to supply produce to the R.N. Barracks,' Mr Ware recalled.

A view of St Budeaux in its rural days.

The ancient King's Tamerton village is seen on the skyline, and included a number of farms, Lynher House and the Georgian manor Mount Tamar, once owned by Colonel John Chard, V.C., of Rorke's Drift fame. Mr Ware thought that the photograph was taken in about 1908 when the house was occupied by General Sir William Wilson. The main landowners, however, were the Trelawny family, who went back to 1639.

The conglomeration of houses seen in St Budeaux include Penzance Villas and Stuart House, Tudor Terrace (now covered by the Co-op store), Florence Street and Trelawny Avenue.

Mrs J. Clarke lived in no. 1 Coldrenick Street with her family for thirty-four years. 'The working men's club is now opposite the house and the back entrance opened to a farm; a relative, Mrs Cann, used to work there for the Luscombe family, delivering milk.'

~ LIFE AT THE ORPHANAGE ~

In the West Devon Records Office is an anonymous written account entitled 'The Life of a Girl in The United Services Orphanage 1907–1916'. This feature is based largely on extracts from that document. The orphanage, now used as offices, stands to this day – a large square building at the top of Albert Road, Devonport.

When this feature originally appeared in the Evening Herald there was still a living link with the orphanage's past in the person of Mrs Winifred Leach, who was 104. She was born at Egloskerry, moved to Plymouth on her father's death and, as a seventeen-year-old, worked as a children's nurse in the United Services orphanage. She remembered that her orphan charges 'were never allowed to be kissed or cuddled'.

The anonymous orphan, in her account, remembered: 'My father had just died, and my mother was left with eight children to bring up, so my elder

HMS *Defiance*.

sister and I were put into the orphanage. I was seven years old. Our hair was completely cropped off, we were bathed and dressed in orphanage uniform. My number was 71. As it was Saturday we played until tea which consisted of bread which was cut so thick that it was nicknamed "doorsteps", and jam and cocoa. We were not allowed to talk at table.

'After prayers were said we went to bed. At 6 o'clock the next morning the bell went and we had to get up, strip to the waist and wash in cold water, clean our teeth and dress. Downstairs, some of the young children had to clean the cutlery with brick-dust on a board and the other young girls had to clean all the boots and shoes. Breakfast was porridge on three mornings a week and bread and dripping on other days.

'After afternoon school, if it was fine, we were taken for a walk around Devonport Park until 5 p.m. As I got older I was allocated to different work to be trained for Domestic Science. Each girl did six months in each department ... bedmaking and polishing floors with Ronuk; preparing meals; and laundry work. We had to stoke the furnaces to keep the water hot, this was very much on the lines of a furnace on a ship. We also had to clear the clinkers out with huge long-handled shovels and rakes. When all the clothes had been boiled in two huge coppers with soda and washing soap, it was blued in tubs of cold water and then put through huge wringers.

'On Sundays we went to church twice a day, also Good Friday morning and Christmas Day. At the age of 15 years every girl was confirmed, for which we wore special white dresses and cloaks which we had to make ourselves.'

The anonymous orphan wrote that after church on Christmas Day, 'when we came home, dinner had been set by members of the staff and committee, who waited on us at table. We had poultry, brussels sprouts, potatoes, and Christmas pudding with lashes of cream. Beside each girl's plate was an orange, apple, nuts, sweets and two crackers, also a brand new silver sixpence given by members of the Committee.

'On the first Monday in the New Year we had a marvellous Christmas tree from which every girl (there were 144) received a lovely gift supplied by the Committee and the Navy. The soldiers and sailors then gave us a marvellous entertainment in the schoolroom.

'If there was a ship launch in Devonport Dockyard, the Navy fetched us all to be present. A few of us were then given a piece of rope.

'Each summer, the Earl and Countess of Mount Edgcumbe invited us over to their house. The Navy took us in their launches. The younger children were met with wagonettes and taken up. On reaching the house we sat on the lawn and ate a pasty (which we girls had made the day before) and each of us had a bottle of lemonade. We had donkey rides which the Earl and Countess had arranged to be there for us. Our tea, also provided by the Earl and Countess, consisted of strawberries and cream, jam and cream puffs, cakes, tea and milk for the younger children. We were very sorry when the time came for us to leave, and the Navy came in their launches to take us home.'

After this feature appeared in the Herald, there came out of the blue an unexpected letter – from Mrs J. Breed. 'My mother, Florence Sweet, née Hann, was the anonymous orphan you quoted,' she explained. 'I wrote the memoirs on behalf of my mother at the request of Mr Woodberry who was the librarian at Efford Library in 1970.'

Florence went into 'service' when she left the orphanage, and married in 1922. She died only a few years ago, aged ninety, and, said her daughter, although she had a rough start to her life she always maintained it was 'good for her'.

The article evoked a flood of memories from former orphans, not least from Mrs Jean Wakeham who was there between 1935 and 1948. Her letter contained some wonderful descriptive touches: 'From the age of nine we had to do all our own mending and knit our own stockings (black) and gloves, on four needles. They were so old after many washings that they turned green ... Yes, there was bullying, but on the whole we all stuck up for each other.'

Mrs Doris Trigger (formerly Gilpin) was there from 1928 until 1937, for part of the time with her two sisters, Rose and Violet. 'Life was very hard, but we made lovely friends ... Miss Glinn, who was a member of the committee and lived opposite in Stoke Terrace with her companion, Miss Howard, saw all the girls on leaving and gave each one a small keepsake. I still have mine.'

The orphans holidayed in Newquay at two-yearly intervals. 'We used to go down in two halves, our trains bringing one party back and taking the others down; we used to pass each other round about Par. There used to be some excitement and a lot of cheering as we passed,' recalled Mrs Trigger.

Christmas time was, as we saw from Florence Sweet's account, a very special time, with the Christmas tree day usually held on 6 January (Twelfth Night). The huge tree held 144 presents, one for each girl. Glorious parties were held at the R.N. Barracks and at H.M.S. Defiance, along with children from Nazareth House and the Royal Dockyard orphanages.

Mrs Trigger, in her seventies, and blessed, as she said, 'with a good but hard life', wrote down the numbers 1 to 144 and was trying to fill in the names of each girl. What a wonderful reunion there could be!

~ MEMORIES SPANNING 105 YEARS OF HISTORY ~

A few years ago I talked to Mrs Lily Type, then 105 years old and living in a residential home in east Devon. Her memories make a nostalgic journey back through all the decades of this century and into the last century; in fact, she recalled the Devonport and Torpoint of the early 1900s as if she had sauntered through their gas-lit streets only the previous day.

She was born at Rose Down Cottage, Tamerton Foliot in July, 1884. Her father took a post as coachman at Derriford House, then one of the area's stately homes. The sprawling parkland with lakes, now the site of Derriford Hospital and its surroundings, was part of the 120-acre estate owned by the Radcliffe family.

Jimmy Love's
emporium, Devonport.

Mrs Type's first memories were of herself as a child of six walking the three miles to the highly regarded village school at Compton Gifford, where she learned to dislike sums – 'I used to hate the blooming things' – but enjoyed spelling, dictation and essay writing. Still, she left school a year early, at fourteen, after the much-loved headmaster, a Mr Roberts, drowned while on holiday.

'I was going to go back again for another year, but somehow I couldn't face it, knowing what had happened to him He used to come around to us pupils and speak on an individual, personal basis. He would help and advise each of us in a kindly way and it made all the difference. I was very fond of school, and if I had to stay home because of sickness I used to get pretty well mad about it. Three miles there and three miles home again might seem a long way, but my two brothers also went with me; they were in the downstairs part of the school.'

When she was fifteen, in 1899, Lily Hocking, as she was then, followed in her father's footsteps by agreeing to work for the Radcliffe family at Derriford estate, as a nursemaid. 'I had the two small girls to look after in the nursery. There was a fully fledged nurse in overall charge and those children would certainly do what she told them. I used to dress, wash and bath them, take them out for walks, help them on to their ponies, and later horses, and sleep with them in the nursery. We would play in one of the streams and pick up hazelnuts from the drive, now part of Derriford Hospital grounds.'

She recalled that the Radcliffes were a very happy family, hospitable and concerned for other people. 'They were great entertainers, sometimes acting as host to up to fifty guests. My mother used to come up and help on those occasions.'

After a few years she changed jobs and became a lady's companion to an old woman in Delgany Villas, but then returned to her former kind of work, taking charge of a nursery in another house just down the road.

She met her future husband, Percy, while attending her own brother's wedding and the couple were married at Eggbuckland parish church in 1912. They set up house at Four Pole Terrace, Torpoint, just two years before the First World War, which was to change everything.

'My husband had to work at Invergordon on the repair and maintenance of warships, so I and my eldest daughter, Marion, went up there to be with him. But it was so cold we came back home for every winter, and it took two days and a night by train to do so.' This was to be her last permanent link with the area until 1954, when she and her husband moved to Exminster. In 1920 the family moved to Manchester where Mr Type worked at what is now the G.E.C. plant.

Mrs Type recalled the outbreak of the Boer War in 1899 when, as a teenager, she heard someone shouting in the Torpoint streets: 'The war with the Boers is on.' 'We thought the end of the world had come. My brother, Frank, served throughout that war and, fortunately, came out of it in one piece.'

Another big event she remembers clearly was the death of Queen Victoria, in 1901. 'I had seen her, quite close at hand, on one of her visits to Plymouth, some years previously, when we had walked five miles into the town centre to catch a glimpse. She looked exactly like you saw in her pictures. Anyway, when she died everyone went into black. If you had a white button on you were expected to replace it with a black one.'

The family used to walk from Devonport, after arriving by the Torpoint ferry, to Crownhill, five miles distant, to see her mother, with her husband carrying their daughter on his shoulder. 'We could not afford a lot of anything, with my husband on low wages at the Dockyard. Special treats were a trip to The Hoe to watch a Punch and Judy Show or, occasionally, to the Eddystone Lighthouse. The Devonport store we all loved was Jimmy Love's in Catherine Street.'

Mrs Type had a special memory of the Evening Herald: 'My mother used to get that every night and then we used to have to be quiet while she read it all out to us during the evening. It was our only contact with the outside world.'

~ MAJESTIC OCEAN LINERS ~

The photograph shows the Mauretania serenely steaming through Plymouth Sound. She was just one of many ocean-going liners that were regular visitors to Plymouth earlier this century.

Mr A. Neetesonne quickly recognised the Mauretania – not surprisingly, because his grandfather worked on the liners, helping to shift passengers' luggage. Often among the passengers were visiting stars, such as Bing

Crowds watch as the *Mauretania* steams into Plymouth Sound.

Crosby and Florence Desmond. He commented: 'Plymouth was a lovely place, with the Navy, the liners and Sunderland flying-boats; it was an afternoon's entertainment for nothing.'

Fred Nicholls said that although the Mauretania called regularly, she was not such a frequent visitor as the French Blue Riband holder, Normandie. He recalled that passengers were taken off the liners to Millbay Docks by the tenders Sir Richard Grenville or Sir Francis Drake.

'My wife watched the Queen Mary come in from the staircase windows of this house [in Peverell Terrace]. She called at Plymouth because there was a strike on at Southampton, her usual port,' he added.

Mr G.G. Lugg pointed out that the Mauretania held the Blue Riband for four different years from 1908. 'I lived "over the shop", or the Cunard shipping office, at 2 Mount Pleasant Terrace, Millbay Road, from the mid 1920s until it was blitzed in 1941. I frequently made trips on the tenders into the Sound and Cawsand Bay to meet the liners. Often there were V.I.P.s landing and I used to carry my autograph book with me.'

Syd Smith commented that Plymouth people loved seeing the liners arrive in the years between the two world wars. Many of the ships were lit up at night, he recalled, with light streaming through the two-and-a-half-inch thick portholes.

Another reader, B. LeBearn, suggested that, judging by the hats, the picture was taken in the early 1930s. 'In those days it was a regular sight to see the ocean-going liners stopping off in the Sound with the mail, and with passengers rushing to make an extra day in London.'

Obviously, the days of these stately ocean liners hold many fond memories for Plymothians.

~ *THE PIER IN ITS HEYDAY* ~

Plymouth's old pier will never rise again but neither will it ever die in the hearts and affections of many elderly local people. Gladys Williams, for instance, remembered it 'with great affection'. She was born in Devonport in 1904, moving to Kingsbridge in 1934 after her husband died.

She pointed out that the pier was popular with 'all classes', not least because of its afternoon and evening concert parties, with an orchestra or a band on Sundays. The winter dances, too, were a great attraction. She remembered going to one on New Year's Eve when she wore a beautiful, full-length pink satin dress: 'Oh, yes – I was going to be the Belle of the Ball.'

But things went wrong. 'Alas, it snowed! By the time I walked the length of the pier and down the six steps to its pavilion the snow and ice were solid on the soles of my shoes!'

That particular evening ended with Mrs Williams 'nearly performing the splits' as she tried to make the ladies' cloakroom via the polished dance floor. Two good Samaritans tried to rescue her and all three crashed to the ground! Eventually, they hoisted her on their shoulders and took her to the cloak-room to the cheers of other dancers. 'But I still had a lovely evening,' she insisted.

On a more serious note, Mrs Williams also remembered the days when the cry went up, 'The Fleet's in!' She observed: 'In those days it was away for

Plymouth's pier is still fondly remembered.

two-and-a-half years – my own father was once in China for that time. We gathered on the pier and at Rusty Anchor and all along the walls to cheer the men home. They were lining the sides at strict attention, with the band on board usually playing, with the flags flying and the pennants streaming aloft.'

Mrs Williams also remembered several slot machines selling a bar of Nestle's or Fry's chocolate for a penny. 'On another machine you turned a handle and watched "What the Butler Saw". Another, more popular, machine depicted the Folies Bergères with girls doing the can-can. There was always a gentleman watching that one, with a few others waiting very discreetly for their turn.'

Finally, Mrs Williams recalled, with obvious delight, the pleasure boats which came from Turnchapel and Phoenix Way to pick up more passengers from the pier for a trip up the Tamar – always very popular.

Wrestling on the pier was the attraction for Mr A.J. Neetesonne. He remembered that, around 1935, top of the bill was a wrestler called King Kong fighting an opponent called Anaconda, a big Canadian.

'I think everyone in Plymouth wanted to see the fight. When my uncle and I arrived there was a queue about one-and-a-half miles long, so we decided to go fishing. We had nothing to fish with but, still, we were on the pier for tuppence. Suddenly a lone door opened and out came a French wrestler. We just sat in a spare seat and saw the whole show without queueing.'

~ THE HARVEST HOME ~

The Harvest Home, set at the busy junction of Tavistock Road and Pound Street, must have been one of Plymouth's best-loved hostelries. You could even tether your horse there overnight in the old days.

Horace Edwards worked there in the 1930s as a barman. His hours would make people gasp today – 8 a.m. to 3 p.m., 5.45 p.m. to 11 p.m. on Saturdays and to midnight on Sundays.

'We had to start at 7 a.m. Tom, the other barman, and I had to hose down the outside of the pub and a by-law said this had to be finished by 8 a.m.,' he recalled. 'I had a half-day on Tuesdays, with every other Sunday night off. The wages were 15 shillings a week after twelve months, rising to £1. I left in 1936 to join the Navy, but they were happy days.'

Another reader who worked in the Harvest Home was Mr R.R.B. Harvey. He was there until November 1940, when he left to join the NAAFI, with which he stayed for forty-three years. He had arrived in Plymouth to work for the then landlord, Mr Langmaid, who had also run the London Inn in Devonport.

Mrs Stacey ran the pub with her husband George Cox from 1948 to 1961. She said that many servicemen would make the Harvest Home their rendezvous when they returned from abroad. 'It was also a very popular pub

The view towards the Old Post Office from the site of the Harvest Home. At one time a familiar landmark, the Harvest Home stood at the junction of Tavistock Road and Pound Street.

for most Plymothians and near the Western National starting point for the Torquay and Exeter buses,' she continued. 'The Americans used to call it the Harvest Moon.'

When Peter Stedman was a boy the Harvest Home had flashing coloured lights on its front elevation. 'On the pillar beside the entrance gates to the yard, shown clearly in the photo, was a bell with the sign "Ring for Ostler". As a schoolboy I used to wonder if a short man with bandy legs dressed in a collarless shirt, breeches and braces would come out if I rang the bell. Only I never had a horse!'

Mr G. Skilton remembered that around the corner in Cobourg Street used to be the Ostler Bell and Cobblestones where farmers tied up their horses while they enjoyed a little refreshment, light or otherwise. Travellers also used to tether their horses there overnight. The stables had cobbled floors in those days.

Mr Skilton also recalled that former Argyle star Raymond Bowden ran his sports shop to the right of the Harvest Home.

~ *THE 'VILLAGE' OF CROWNHILL* ~

Crownhill is still referred to as 'the village' by many older residents, some of whose families have been shopping in the stores shown in these photographs for generations.

Mrs Denis McShane's family moved to Crownhill in 1939 and lived in the police house attached to the police station and the library; her father was the 'village' sergeant. Recognising Stentiford's bakery, shown in the top photograph on the next page, she recalled that the owner used to open it on Sunday mornings so that his customers could take their dinners to be cooked in the ovens.

Crownhill's well-known shops.

One of the main streets in Crownhill.

'Farther up the road towards Plumer Barracks, Mrs Naylor and her mother had a grocery shop. A fish and chip shop adjoined this, then a butcher, two private houses – one of which later had the downstairs converted into a hair-dressers – while Isbells sweet shop was on the corner.'

Mrs McShane said that the post office later became Churchill's the fish-mongers and then a chemist. She also remembered that Davis' Garage was on the opposite corner to the post office, with Motleys wool shop and Bowmans vegetable shop, next to the Tamar Hotel – "with dear Mr Ponsford!"

Chapman's Garage was opposite the police station, and on the other corner of Cross Park was a dairy which later became a chemist. Mr and Mrs Lavers ran a barbers and hairdressing business and Mr and Mrs Davis looked after the newsagents, later taken on by the Pascoe family.

'On the other corner, going up towards Luckes Garage, was a butchers, Shackerley's greengrocery shop and, later, the Goodbody's bakery and shop/snack bar. I still live in Crownhill and, to this day, my family refer to "going to the village" when they go to the shops,' added Mrs McShane.

Stanley Searle pointed out that John Pascoe, owner of the newsagents, was a well-known figure on the city council for many years. 'In the early years of this century, one of the shops was owned by Mr William Martin, a brother of my maternal grandfather. It was called Tamar Dairy, and if not next door, certainly close to the Tamar Hotel. I can remember being taken to the shop by my grandfather when I was a boy, then living in the Stoke area, around 1918–20.'

Another reader, M.L. Sutton, who worked in Dingles vegetable shop in 1949, remembered that fresh fruit was brought out every day from the market. She also remembered a dental practice run from a private house and observed that 'the street has not altered much'.

~ *PLUMER BARRACKS* ~

The photograph shows the old Plumer Barracks in Crownhill. According to one Herald reader, Mr A. W. Phillips, the view is taken from west to east.

'The troops in the foreground are actually across the main road through the village, in the west side of the Barracks. The establishment was in two parts across the then main Tavistock to Plymouth Road. Traffic was frequently held up while troops crossed from one side to the other.'

Mr Phillips thought that the building on the right was part of the main guardroom, now occupied by Plumer House and Crownhill Court. Reg Harris, another reader, believed that the building behind the left-hand gatepost was used as a library until it was demolished in 1991.

Plumer Barracks, Crownhill.

Mrs A.W. Smith recalled that the Worcestershire Regiment used to be stationed at Plumer. She met her husband when he was an officers' groom there over sixty years ago.

ONE PENNY RETURN ON THE OLD PUFFING BILLY

'The train approaching platform one is the 9.25 from Friary, calling at Oreston and Turnchapel': this was a familiar announcement through the loudspeaker at Pomphlett station in the 1930s, when the 'Turnchapel Express' noisily chuffed its way over the old swing bridge over the Plym.

It was a sight fondly remembered by several readers, one of whom remarked that it cost one penny return for a child to travel from Friary to Oreston. No wonder it was so popular, as Mr F.G. Frampton observed: he used the train for a day out to Jennycliff beach.

Roy Boyner remembered being taken by his grandparents on the train in the 1920s, during the holidays from Salisbury Road school. They boarded it at Lucas Terrace halt in Tothill. 'We walked up the hill to Jennycliff or Bovisand, a big event in those days. I loved trains.'

Mr G. Skilton pointed out that in the photograph the train had just passed Bailey's timber yard, on its right, then more commonly known as Pickle Yard. 'Timber boats came into the middle of the Cattewater. They unloaded their cargo, chained together, into the water, when it was towed by the tug Alice to Pickle Yard. The timber, taken to different areas, was used as sleepers for the lines.'

Mr Skilton reckoned that the photo was taken in the summer or on a bank holiday, because of its four carriages. 'It only pulled so many on such special occasions. Normal service was two carriages.'

Steam on the
Turnchapel line, 1924.

~ ALL STATIONS TO SALTASH ~

Mr Ware's goods yard. Alongside is the steamship S.S. *Saxon* one of the many vessels using the quay, providing access to Wolseley road, with its cargo of 650 tons of coal, discharged by a team of 12 stevedores.

It cost just three old pence to travel by train from St Budeaux to the heart of Plymouth about eighty years ago. Local historian Marshall Ware, who has written two books on St Budeaux, remembered going to school by train and hopping off at the old Mutley station; in those days Plymouth had a highly intricate rail network and numerous stations.

Mr Ware could remember when there were thirty trains a day, both ways, between Millbay and Saltash, particularly popular with commuters because

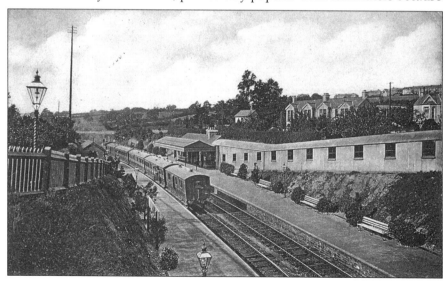

Mr Tolley's domain, 1892.

25

they called at St Budeaux Ferry Road, Keyham and Devonport, among other local stations.

'I started using the railway in 1918 to get to school at Plymouth College. That train left St Budeaux Victoria Road and went to Friary and Mutley, which is where I got off. Oddly enough, it started its journey from London Waterloo, but became a "local" when it reached Plymouth. Of course, all the trains stopped at St Budeaux in those days.'

Mr Ware recalled that the Victoria Road station, St Budeaux's first, opened on 2 June 1890, built by the Plymouth, Devonport and South-West Junction Railway, and 'worked up' by the old London and South Western line. 'The first train down from Waterloo on the opening day arrived promptly on time, at 7.20 a.m. It was greeted by a bevy of local worthies. The station master was Mr Edmund Tolley, who lived right by his place of work. The vicar, the Reverend William Green, arranged for the church bells to be rung that evening in celebration.'

The signal box was fully functional, manned by a staff of two, and the present car park is the site of what was once a very busy goods yard. Mr Ware's father held a lease of the goods yard at an annual rent of £16 for his coal business and as a carrier agent.

The first 'up' train for Salisbury, at 7.20 a.m., carried the mail bags from the Devonport post sorting office. Postmaster Mr Ozias Currin collected the mail which was sorted at no. 50 Victoria Road, now a boot and shoe shop. The postal clerk was Mrs Beatrice Mitchell, formerly Hammett, who remembered Mrs Currin the postmistress, sending off telegrams by morse code.

Very little remains to remind anyone of the L. & S.W. railway other than an old solid iron boundary marker which is in Mr Ware's garden, still in pristine condition. Deeply embedded in the ground, it weighs half a hundredweight and indicated the extent of the railway boundaries.

The goods yard was an important depot for deliveries of fertilisers to Tamerton and the Bere Alston peninsula, but during the First World War its importance rose further. 'My father, a carriers' agent as well as a coal merchant, had to handle the goods trains coming down from the Midlands to deliver shell cases. These were then taken to the Bull Point armaments depot by horse and cart for filling with explosives before being taken out to ships. He, and three other carriers, had to work almost day and night to handle all those. They shifted 1,309 tons in 1915 and 4,052 the following year. My father was fuel controller for the area during the war, which was why he resigned from Devonport Town Council in 1914, the year it was merged into Plymouth's.'

St Budeaux's other station, the G.W.R. at Ferry Road, did not open until 1 June 1904, and it soon became very busy because it was on the Saltash to Millbay line. This suburban service really opened up Plymouth for St Budeaux people who had to pay only 3d. each way to get into the heart of the city.

In those days there were four deliveries of mail a day, the last at 5 p.m. A post girl, remembered as something of a beauty with raven-black hair hanging in a cluster of curls on her shapely shoulders, used to deliver the post to the King's Tamerton area.

One of the postmen, a Mr Ford, was a Crimean War veteran with a patch over one eye. He carried a few letters for outlying farmsteads and cottages, in what is now part of the urban sprawl. 'He used to blow a whistle and Mr Bettinson, of the Toll Gate Cottage, at the bottom of Government Road, took some of the letters and passed them on, as opportunity occurred, to passers-by or men employed on the farms,' recounted Mr Ware.

'His principal duty was to carry Service letters to the officers and residents at the barracks and Government offices at Bull Point. I know all this seems exceedingly haphazard in the light of modern methods, but people did get several deliveries a day, some of the letters having been posted only a few hours earlier.'

COLLECTING TRAM TICKETS IN BASKET STREET

This photograph of two trams passing each other in Basket Street triggered off memories for a number of Herald readers. For Arthur Lee, for instance, it was the memory of meeting his first sweetheart 'on the very place where the solitary man is standing on the corner'.

He recalled that Bateman's Corner, as it was known, was a favourite meeting place, 'especially when the young ladies came out from the Spooner's store, across the road, after work'.

Another reader, Mr Haughey, used to walk down that exceedingly narrow 'thoroughfare' into Westwell Street in order to visit the school dentist on the side of Princess Square, almost opposite the gardens. 'There was only enough room for two adults to stand side by side on the narrow pavement, and on the other side room for just one.'

Stella Tucker remembered going to Basket Street every day with her sister to look for tram tickets ending with the figure seven. The reason for this strange excursion was that her eldest sister was having a baby and some wag put it around that these tickets had to be collected before the baby could be born safely. 'We really believed it, too,' she wrote. 'I wonder, now, what they did with all those tickets!'

Mr F.G. Frampton pointed out that the top centre of the photograph was the junction of St Andrew's and Old Town Streets, and also Whimple Street where the Western National had offices.

Mrs R. May was one of several readers who drew attention to Bateman's the opticians, plainly marked by a huge pair of spectacles on the outside of the building, one side of which faced Bedford Street. D. Haskell's the hair-dressing salon was on the first floor. 'I walked from Bedford Street to Bedford Park and back six days a week, from 1938 to 1940, but cannot remember the names of all the shops now,' she added. Mrs J. Curle also knew Haskell's because the owner, Mrs Hurd, was her aunt.

Two trams passing in Basket Street.

~ *ROLL UP AND LISTEN TO THE BAND* ~

'Oh, listen to the band!' they used to say. And regularly on a Sunday morning generations of Plymouth people did just that, at Raglan Barracks pictured here. The public were allowed into 'the Lines', or forecourt, but not into the barracks.

Mr W.J. Dawe pointed out that there were a north and a south barracks, and the line of soldiers in the picture shows the division between the two

sections. The building at the top of the picture was the officers' mess, North Raglan, he said. The building on the right of the photo was a NAAFI club.

Soldiers marching at Raglan Barracks.

Mr G. Baker thought that the picture was taken around 1935 because 'those were the days of knee-length puttees and peaked caps, commonly known as "Cheesecutters". I suspect that the unit shown was the Royal Sussex Regiment – it must have been a unit of the line because they are parading their colours.'

Mr Baker's late father-in-law was at Raglan with the Royal Sussex, so he had something of a 'family feel' for the barracks. He wrote: 'Those were the days of a thousand men in a battalion.' Referring to the motor transport at the top left, he recalled that, at the time, the battalion was receiving the Lloyd armoured carrier, later to be replaced by the 'Bren' carrier. He pointed out that, from 1948 onwards, the barracks became home to many Territorial Army units, including the Royal Signals, Military Police and Royal Engineers.

As a child, Mrs Dorothy Showell recalled, she went along to the barracks, which they knew as 'The Lines', every Sunday morning to watch the soldiers marching. There was usually a different band and a different regiment each week.

Mrs Peggy Hugo also shared some early memories of the barracks, among them a garrison sports day on the adjoining field. 'I must have been only about three and was taken there by my mother's friend, "Aunty Butcher". To this day I remember the sun in my eyes and trying to find my way back to "Aunty" after buying an ice-cream and looking along the rows of laps in order to identify her dress.

'A few years later I remember my brother and I and another boy, Teddy Archer, being taken to the sergeants' mess and playing under a large table there while the fathers imbibed.' These long-remembered visits used to follow watching the parade and listening to the band on a Sunday morning.

~ *CHILDREN'S PARADISE IN CENTRAL PARK* ~

It was an adventure land, a children's paradise, which looked set to last for ever. That was how many people remembered Central Park; in fact, generations of Plymothians spent many happy childhood hours playing there.

The park contained two large pools, one for paddling, the other for model boats. In addition, swings, slides, roundabouts and climbing frames helped to ensure that the area was a children's dream, with no fear of danger. But then vandals began to wreak havoc, damaging the pools so badly that eventually they had to be closed.

Mrs Olive Dickinson remembered the pools being opened in the early 1930s, when she was a child. She recalled the see-saws and, for the more adventurous, a rope roundabout.

'If you had a ha'penny to spend there was a small shop in which you could deliberate between a lollipop, two gob-stoppers or a few sweets – the choice seemed enormous. When eventually we tired of the swings it was down to the field, with its little stream, there to play cowboys and Indians or cops and robbers. Oh, the delight of a simple picnic – the drink made of lemon crystals

Central Park was a haven for children between the two wars.

– on the green, clean grass. My friends and I used to walk from Keyham and back, arriving home tired and happy.'

Another reader, J. Sommers, pointed out that across the path, to the left of the picture, was the site for children's talent competitions on Saturday afternoons, using a wooden stage. 'All the smaller children were asked to go to the front of the audience and sit cross-legged, to listen to the contestants. I believe rewards were 3d., 2d. and 1d.'

Sailing model yachts in the pool was a childhood activity of Jim Kindon, who recounted the ways and means he used to achieve the maximum speed. He attached a long length of string to the bow in order to pull the boat back after it had sailed across to the other side.

'I would tow my yacht back across the pond by running backwards at a great rate of knots, delighting in the high bow wave generated by my craft. You can probably guess what happened. I had failed to recognise that the distance between the two ponds was less than the width of the pond I was sailing on. Reversing at great speed, I proceeded to go full-tilt backwards into pond number two, which brought my afternoon's sailing to an abrupt halt.

'The final humiliation came about when the bus conductor refused to let me aboard his bus because of my soaking wet condition, leaving me with a long walk home to Higher St Budeaux, there to face my mum's displeasure.'

Mrs R. Smith also admitted to having tumbled into the pool. 'I can well remember how uncomfortable I felt sitting in the bus on the way home to St Jude's, with my wet and cold sandals and my cousin's vest beneath my own coat.'

But, of course, childhood memories wouldn't be real without the odd mishap thrown in!

~ THE CO-OP EMPORIUM ~

The massive building shown in the photograph is the old Co-operative Society emporium, situated at the junction of Frankfort and Courtenay Streets. Ted Smith remembered its hall with a large stage and balcony used for concerts and dances. His father was on the Society's education committee and, he added, 'my sister started work in the "check" office in April 1914'.

Christopher Kingdon commented that the store, 'imposing in the style of Harrods', was the best of its kind in Plymouth. The main entrance was in Frankfort Street and opposite another entrance in Courtenay Street was the Co-op's grocery shop, with a cafe on the first floor. 'My mother would take my sister and I to collect her "divi", worth getting in those days,' Mr Kingdon added.

Enid Ware enthused even more about the Co-op: 'It was quite fantastic with its shops, offices and large hall. When I was seventeen my then boyfriend, who worked for the Co-op, asked me to the staff dance. I wore a

The Co-op emporium was an impressive sight in pre-war Plymouth.

pink lace dress with a wide sash and dear Steve said I looked a million dollars!'

Mrs Ware recalled that, after collecting and sticking stamps of various values on to the sheets of sticky paper, 'we would take them to the check office and get 2s. 6d. for every pound. That was really good and a great help to my mother with four children. It bought our shoes. All her shopping was done at the Co-op, so she had a tidy dividend.' Mrs Ware also remembered that the Co-op ran a group called Comrades, a sort of Girl Guide movement.

A regular reader, Mr S. Robertson, pointed out that the store would have been just over 100 years old had it not been destroyed in the Blitz. Mr J.S. Ferris remembered that sad event only too well: he and some fellow Royal Marines helped to salvage tables and other items, stacking them across the road by a church. Sadly, they also came across dozens of children inside the store looting items to take home.

~ *BEDFORD STREET IN THE OLD DAYS* ~

Bedford Street was a well-known part of pre-war Plymouth, shown here with the old Globe Hotel in the background and an Italian circus arriving in grand style.

Christopher Kingdon observed that, unlike now, many people lived in and around the town centre in pre-war days, so it was more lively. 'What a smart area it was around Bedford Street and the adjoining George Street.'

Reg Heggie claimed that the photograph was taken before 1899 because in that year the Prudential building opened on the Globe Hotel site. 'Bedford Street changed very little from the scene in this picture to the time of the Blitz,' he said. Mr S. Robertson pointed out that at one time the Globe was a coaching hotel and the local headquarters of a political party.

Harry Waring picked out the end of Dingles store on the extreme right, with John Yeo's further to the east, but out of the picture. The Bank of England building is seen at the other end, he said, with various small shops in between it and Dingles.

Like many older readers, he could recall the spectacular Christmas grotto scenes which were a feature of that store, Yeo's, Pophams, Spooners and the Co-operative emporium. 'Unemployed men were glad to earn a few bob to

A fleet of fine white horses heads the procession of the Italian circus along Bedford Street.

act as Father Christmas for those few weeks. They had to be of a kindly disposition and they were. Most even managed a twinkle in their eyes when they gave a small present to the children who, in those days, were not so demanding and assertive as today.'

Lilian Hacking remembered her mother buying her brown leather or cloth button-up gaiters, with a strap to go under the shoe, from Dingles. She wore them in the colder months from the time she was six until she was sixteen. 'They cost the equivalent of 75p. They came up to just below the knees and were the warmest, most stylish item of clothing I ever wore around my legs. I used them until the 1950s when, suddenly, they disappeared from the shops.'

~ L.W.S.R. ENGINE No 164 ~

At one time a familiar sight, this engine was owned by the L.S.W.R. Three of these engines were allocated to Plymouth Friary engine shed when it stood at the end of Desborough Road, St Jude's, recalled Mr R. F. Stephens. 'They were used on local freight and passenger duties to Tavistock,' he added. 'Many a young fireman, including myself, learned their trade on these tank engines before doing duty on the main line. They were still in use in the late 1950s. The locomotive in the picture looks as if it had just been delivered because it is in mint condition.'

Mr Stephens identified the engine as a O-4-4T-type tank engine built by Dougal Drummond in the late 1890s. Meanwhile, Walter Eglinton looked into his railway books and discovered that the engine carried 5 ft 7 in. driving wheels, 18 in. by 26 in. cylinders, and 150 lb pressure which could be raised to 175 lb. He pointed out that 105 of its class were built, initially being used to haul the best express trains between Plymouth and Exeter. 'They were powerful and fast,' he observed.

One of the engines used on the Tavistock line (photograph supplied by Mr C.E.B. Dixon).

34

Mr J.F.R. Snell recounted that this engine, achieved a certain notoriety when working a semi-fast Exeter to Plymouth train on 6 March 1898. 'It left the track between Brentor and Tavistock, running for some 200 yards before parting from its seven carriages which, by good fortune, remained in upright position. After this accident the class was restricted to mainly suburban services.'

He mentioned that this particular locomotive was built in June 1897 and was withdrawn from service in 1959. However, one example of this class still works the Swanage railway, apparently.

Mr Eglinton also referred to the accident between Brentor and Tavistock, which became the subject of a Board of Trade enquiry. There, a Colonel Yorke criticised the use of a front-couple tank engine with leading and driving axle loads of 16 and 18 tons respectively. 'But the permanent way was scarcely the sum of excellence. It included 82 lb rails, considerably worn.'

~ THE BRIDGE THEY CALLED THE SWITCHBACK ~

First it was known as the 'Switchback' and then 'Shaky Bridge'. And it carried trains to Waterloo through some of the most delectable countryside in the West. It was, of course, Camel's Head Bridge, crossing Weston Mill lake.

The scene was recognised by many readers. Mr T.H. Adams pointed out that the trams had to stop at that point in their journey for the passengers to get out and walk across before getting into another, waiting tram to take them to St Budeaux and Saltash Passage. He observed that the nearby railway bridge took the old Southern line to Waterloo, via such places as Okehampton and Yeovil.

Eric Dixon recalled that the jetty was used for loading ammunition barges. The creek itself, of course, has long been infilled to provide a car park and access into the north end of the dockyard. 'This was known as the "coal heap", where large stocks of coal were kept for fuelling steam ships,' he commented.

Pat Ghillyer was another one who remembered that the stream ran right up under the wooden bridge to cover the site of the corporation tip, and that barges used to travel up it. 'That wooden structure was known as the "Switchback" bridge because it swayed backwards and forwards when pedestrians used it. Later it was dubbed "Shaky Bridge" and kept that title for some years.' Mr Ghillyer also pointed out that the foreground in the picture covers the site of the future Camel's Head pub, plus a cinema.

Copies of the Evening Herald of 22 and 30 August 1973 were sent in by Reg Bossom, another local reader. One of the newspapers carried memories from Miss Smale, who pointed out that the water mentioned used to go right under the bridge and up to Weston Mill village. Over eighty when she wrote, Miss Smale also remembered when the site of the tram shed was a meadow where 'Cheap Jacks' used to call every Saturday to sell all sorts of oddments.

Camel's Head Bridge, also known as the 'Switchback'.

The other paper carried an item from Mr Bossom, in which he pointed out that the G.W.R. bridge was opened in May 1903. It seems that an 8-foot pathway for foot passengers ran by the side of the railway track, giving almost direct access between Keyham and St Budeaux. In the same paper, Mr R.C. Sambourne was quoted as saying that the Plymouth, Devonport and South-Western junction railway line, shown in the picture, opened in 1891 from Lydford to Devonport. Camel's Head and Weston Mill halts were opened in 1906, he said. The creek, apparently once visible from Ham House grounds, was first bridged by the Cornwall Railway in 1859, the year the Brunel bridge spanning the Tamar opened.

~ *STATION OF THE STARS* ~

Millbay Station was the starting point for liner passengers on their way to Paddington by boat train during the inter-war years. Many Hollywood stars, including Charlie Chaplin, Norma Shearer and George Raft, began their trip in England at Millbay, along with tens of thousands of less famous visitors.

The station also served such local spots as Yelverton, Princetown, Launceston and Tavistock, as many readers recalled on seeing the photograph. The site is now covered by the chunky ugliness of Plymouth Pavilions, but memories of the station's heyday live on.

As Mr S. Robertson pointed out, it was 'one of the gateways to England. The tracks that ran into the docks must have transported almost every V.I.P. to London after arriving from, say America. I read that a gang of Irish navvies put all the tracks in place over a weekend when it was being built,' he added.

Mr R.P. Bromidge knew all about the station – he worked there in the thirties. 'Although the traffic was in decline by then,' he said, 'it was still a very busy station with several special services running, including valuable connections with such liners as the two Queens and the French Normandie, the passengers from which were brought to Millbay by tenders.'

He added that passengers for Paddington were catered for by the provision of Boat Specials, which were shunted into the docks and given priority of track. There was also very important traffic from P & O liners, whose cargo included spice and gold bars, brought from the docks in a horse-drawn covered cart. 'This was unloaded in the forecourt on to the flat-topped trolley and taken to the bullion van which, when loaded, was then shunted to the front of the London train.'

Mr Bromidge pointed out that the thirties were dangerous times. 'It was said that some of the passengers, young "domestics" from the Continent, and students, were suspected of spying for Germany.'

Thomas Taylor, who observed that Millbay was closed to passengers early in 1971, was a member of the famous Ballard Institute, just along the road. He and his pals often had to wait while a train from the docks crossed Millbay Road en route to the station. 'Often it would be carrying notabilities, such as film stars, etc., who landed at Plymouth and who were brought to the docks by the tenders Hawkins and Raleigh.'

Christopher Kingdon thought that Millbay should have been called Plymouth Central because it was so handy for locals and visitors, and so near to the hotels, cinemas and shops. 'One only had to come out and turn left into the short Station Road to be in Union Street. It was the days of the L.N.E.R. and the L.M.S. The sixpenny Woolworth trains for the moors, calling at North Road and Mutley stations, were so popular that I've been crammed into the guard's van coming home.'

Mr F.G. Frampton suggested that the picture was taken from the nearby Continental Hotel where he worked as a page boy in 1936. Adding to the scene, Stanley Griffin pointed out that Millbay Park lay in the background (remember the old Devon Wednesday League matches there?) and that opposite was the stately Duke of Cornwall Hotel, reminding us of some of Plymouth's pre-war architectural splendours.

RIDING ON THE BUFFERS OF THE HORSE-DRAWN TRAMS

This photograph of the old Princess Square area drew a large response from Herald readers. George Horwell thought that the tram had just left Princess Square and, near Lockyer Street, was about to turn left at Derry's Clock. Westwell Street was on the left.

Mr A. Ruse, a vigorous eighty-seven when he wrote, well remembered riding with his brothers on the big buffers of the horse-drawn trams from

A tram in the area of Princess Square.

Plymbridge to the terminus outside the Theatre Royal. 'Those were the days, too, of the D'Oyly Carte and Carl Rosa opera companies, very popular in Plymouth.'

Mrs M. Adams commented on the partly demolished Central Hotel, at the corner of Lockyer Street. 'It brought back many memories for me,' she said. 'My late father, Charles Jenkins, was a member of the staff for many years until it was taken over by the post office in the late 1930s. A newspaper cutting of the time strangely comments: "It will be no consolation to know that the building erected on the site is evidence of the growing popularity of the telephone service." '

Mrs Adams pointed out that St Catherine's Church was opposite the hotel on the left, though out of sight in the picture, with the much-loved Repertory Theatre on the far corner.

An unusual response came from Fred Matthews, who commented that it was about this time and place that Oswald Moseley's notorious Blackshirts 'came under fire'. It's hard to think of the Blackshirts cutting much ice in Plymouth, with its somewhat diffident attitude to political extremists of all kinds.

~ *CHINA-CLAY WAGONS AT LAIRA* ~

The Crabtree Inn area of Laira has changed dramatically since this picture was taken. Mr George Horwell pointed out that the inn was situated between the Embankment and Marsh Mills and was eventually demolished to make way for the new road.

Laira in the Edwardian era.

The picture brought back happy memories for Mrs Alice McMahon. She could remember 'lovely summer evening walks taken regularly along this now busy road at Marsh Mills which, in pre-war days, was so much prettier'.

Mr F.G. Frampton observed that the old china clay line for Plymbridge is on the left of the picture. And James Williams was involved with the horses which pulled the wagons along it, from Plymbridge to the jetty at Prince Rock.

'There were nine teams of them. Each pulled five wagons. Crossing the main line at Laira was a bit hairy, but all the drivers had good judgement.' Mr Williams is, in fact, the sole remaining driver, so he was naturally pleased to see the picture.

Enid Ware recognised the scene because her grandmother lived in the old Laira village, the tip of which is seen on the horizon.

~ WHEN THE FLOODS CAME TO LAIRA ~

Rowing up the avenue on a rainy afternoon! No, this isn't the title of an old George Formby 'hit' but a memory sparked by this photograph of Laira. It was one of several reminiscences supplied by a reader who spent what appears to have been a delightfully happy and carefree childhood in that eastern suburb.

Part of Laira when it was still undeveloped.

Mrs Phyllis Bartrop claimed she could name everyone who lived there from the mid 1920s to the 1930s – some feat of memory! She went on to name

a few of them, recalling that the local postman, Mr Joy, and his family lived in the first house shown on the right. Mr and Mrs Mitchell ran the corner shop from their bungalow, the next dwelling along.

'My school friends lived in the first house on the left and our chimney-sweep next door,' recalled Mrs Bartrop. 'We used to ride on the clay-truck's bumpers and go right out to Plymbridge and back again. I shudder now to think of the risks we used to take. We didn't have TV in those days but life was never dull.'

She dipped further into her rich store of memories by relating how she and her friends went to the Band of Hope classes in a chapel that used to be situated at the bottom of the school's hill. On Monday they trooped off to the local Co-operative Society's classes in Laira Green School. In addition, there were Guides and Brownies and, at the church, what were known as the King's Messengers, with a Reverend Strong in charge.

An occasional bout of unexpected excitement would surface, as when two convicts, Messrs Gaskin and Mullan, escaped from Dartmoor prison. There was no hope of Phyllis and her young friends going to bed early that night. 'We stayed up all night watching the police with their lamps flashing and their whistles blowing.'

When the nearby River Plym overflowed its banks, Phyllis couldn't sit glued to the goggle-box watching it all happen. Much better than that – she and her friends rowed a boat up the flooded avenues, thoroughly enjoying themselves in the simple, unspoilt way that the children of her generation did.

Another reader who remembered Laira when it was still undeveloped was Mrs Pat Howarth. She lived in the bungalow on the right of the picture for the first four years of her married life, about fifty years ago. She recalled that the railway ran in front, with gates that opened on to a crossing.

~ THE THEATRE ROYAL AND ITS SURROUNDINGS ~

Behind the familiar sight of Derry's Clock, many readers identified the old Theatre Royal and, further on, the Athenaeum. The scene was a focal point for memories of the charm of old Plymouth.

Mr S. Robertson worked at the Royal Hotel, adjoining the theatre, for a few days only as a young waiter in the grill room. His employment soon ended, he recalled, because 'my parents drew the line at my working from 8 a.m. to 2 p.m. and then from 4 p.m. to midnight'.

He pointed out that the bus or tram inspectors' small office is seen perched over the underground toilets and that opposite this, on the right, was an arcade which ran into Union Street.

Ken Gardiner thought that the suspended umbrella sign, near the bottom of George Street, marked the Limpenny shop. He recalled that the 'very posh' Palm Court Orchestra played at the Royal and that the indoor corridor leading to the bar/lounge was lined with beautiful plants.

A familiar sight in pre-war Plymouth: Derry's Clock and, behind it, the Theatre Royal.

Mrs Diane Joyce knew all about the old Athenaeum because her great-aunt and uncle were caretakers there. Referring to the two round lodges in the distance, either side of the entrance to the Crescent, she recalled further family associations. 'In the mid-1930s my great-grandfather, Charles Capley Spurr, was the gardener at The Crescent and, with my great-grandmother, Rhoda, lived in the two lodges, one of which they used as a bedroom, the other as a lounge. My mother remembers seeing all their furniture sticking out at angles because of the round walls.' Mrs Joyce recalled that the local children used to steal conkers from the grounds, 'and grandad would chase them on his little short legs, and they would shout "grasshopper" after him'.

It was inevitable that someone would mention Genoni's Swiss Cafe, opposite the Royal. It was a favourite meeting place for generations of Plymothians, not least at 'elevenses', and it offered a splendid service. Mrs Kathleen Mills remembered Genoni's and also recalled many of the big-time shows at the former Royal, such as White Horse Inn, Wild Violets and Sunny. She particularly mentioned a play, The Miracle, in which Eve Foster stood still for about 45 minutes portraying the Blessed Virgin Mary.

'A word, too, for the wonderful pantomimes with their superb scenery and the various transformations changing before our very eyes. All pantos had their speciality act. One was done by Chinese acrobats when all the theatre lights came on as they climbed, one on top of the other. We also got entertainment in the long undercover passages which went up to the gallery, such as a man with a banjo, paper-tearers doing wonders with newspapers and Teddy Weeks Cough-no-More drops at 1d. a packet!'

Reg Heggie pointed out that no tramlines or electric overhead cables are shown in the picture, which led him to suggest that it was taken before the 1870s. At that time, he said, a Hansom cab rank stood above the public conveniences. The small hexagonal hut was at that time the rest room for drivers.

Mrs E. Fedrick recalled that the area marked the old tram terminus. 'This reminds me of our days of poverty,' she wrote. 'My father was killed in the First World War. I last saw him when I was five. The pension my mother received was £1 a week for herself and 10 shillings (50p) for me, until I was fourteen.

'One year we went to town to do some Christmas shopping. After spending the few shillings we had managed to save, we wondered if we had enough left to ride home. We found we had just over tuppence ha'penny and the fare from the theatre to Peverell was one-and-a-half pence. So we had to walk to Drake Circus and pay 1d. each!'

Mrs Fedrick also said that she used to feel like a pauper when she looked at the ladies arriving at the theatre. 'They arrived in horse-drawn cabs, arrayed in beautiful long evening dresses, with white ermine coats or capes.'

~ SHOPS IN FRANKFORT STREET ~

Frankfort Street was near the hub of the city before the Second World War. The area bounded by Frankfort, Cornwall, Russell and Bedford Streets contained a vast array of shops and stores. One was Coster's departmental store, almost next door to the Evening Herald office and Underhill's the stationers, clearly seen in the picture.

Like so many readers, Mr E.S. Stoward had a personal involvement. He worked for ten years as a local deliverer with a handcart. 'One of my tasks was to collect the Western Morning News each day for Sir Frederick Winnicot. I had many a push by the constable at the junction shown in the

Frankfort Street appears to be a hive of activity in this pre-war photograph.

picture. I left the job in 1940 to join the R.A.F., and my wife enlisted in the W.R.N.S.'

Jeanne Curle spotted King Street in the distance. She recalled a shoe shop on the top right corner and, further down, Jerome's the photographers, Pelosis' ice-cream and then the old Odeon cinema, formerly the Regent. The cinema had a seating capacity of over 3,200. Mr S. Robertson thought that the shoe shop, mentioned by Mrs Curle, was Oliver's.

Mrs June Watts remembered that the old Regent cinema was in Frankfort Buildings and occupied the area now taken up roughly by Littlewood's. The adjacent stores were Snell's the motor-cycle shop, Harry Limsdell's, barber, and Jack Heard the butcher. Mrs Watts said: 'I can be so positive because I was born at no. 2 Frankfort Buildings.'

George Horn mentioned that the back of the cinema was opposite the Barley Sheaf in Cambridge Street and nearby was a cut-meat shop. 'Further up Cambridge Street was Spence's the newsagents and, below, one of the many pubs. I used to live in King Gardens where Evans the newsagents was on one corner and a post office on the other,' he recalled.

As a boy he belonged to the St John Ambulance cadet corps attached to the Odeon. 'The S.J.A.B. corps took part in a film about the work. We also did first aid duty on The Hoe, where the Dome is now situated, and at Home Park when Argyle were playing.'

~ PIN LANE ~

This photograph of Pin Lane, on The Barbican, is taken looking towards Southside Street. One reader, J. Sommers, pointed out that the houses seen on the right each had two doors – one at ground-floor level and the other up the steps to the first floor.

Pin Lane, one of Plymouth's oldest streets.

Frank Tucker lived in the area during the war and recalled many exciting and happy years there. He remembered the bombing of Green Street and Stillman Street and the air-raid shelters. 'Then there were those marvellous Sunderland flying-boats in the Sound. What a sight they were!'

Mr Tucker obviously enjoyed his war as a boy, for he concluded by saying that all those 'great days' were brought to an end when he was evacuated to South Wales!

~ LIFE AS AN A.R.P. WARDEN ~

Dancing the nights away on Plymouth Hoe, while the nearby city centre was a wrecked shambles, is one of the memories that former A.R.P. warden Elsie Burnett said would always stay with her. Elsie Ellis, as she was then, remembered that hundreds of people, casting off their wartime cares, gathered up there to dance to the bright beat of favourite bandleaders like Ted Coleman, Frankie Fuge and others.

'Even though we were at war, we had our good times,' she said. 'There was no covetousness. We shared everything, including our free time, and the Hoe

Looking at the bomb damage down Frankfort Street towards King Street, near Elsie Burnett's old home.

dances were immensely popular.' Mrs Burnett recalled that these provided opportunities to meet Servicemen from many different countries, in a happy spirit. 'We always made for The Hoe in the summer – it was impossible to go anywhere on outings, as such.'

On colder evenings, Mrs Burnett and her friends would make for the Guildhall where Billy Mitchell and New Imperials were among the visiting bands. When that was bombed they switched to the Corn Exchange and the large hall at the Co-operative store in Raleigh Street.

Mrs Burnett had enlisted in the A.R.P. when she was eighteen and soon became familiar with the most searing sights. There was the time when the pub The Grapes, at the end of Neswick Street, was destroyed at the same time that Cecil Street was bombed, and the houses all around her own were destroyed. A young Serviceman on leave standing in a nearby doorway was killed by the blast.

She patrolled in the area near the old railway arch which used to straddle Union Street. 'We went out in twos, and with we women would be a man. I agree very much with other people who say that Plymouth people took the Blitz well. We all had to just get on with things, whatever sights we had seen that caused us horror.'

However, many of the sights and sounds of those days are indelibly etched on her mind. They include the baled-out German pilot hanging in a tree on the Blockhouse, and the memory of a family who lived at the end of Cecil Street being wiped out. 'We saw people in the shelters covered with blood and, sometimes, with pieces of their limbs missing.

'Come Christmas, and the party spirit resurfaced in the shelters, which were duly decorated for the occasion. We exchanged gifts, had a knees-up, enjoyed by all.' Mrs Burnett's parents refused to go to the shelters, like many other people, and would just lie in bed or crouch in the passage.

When she wasn't on patrol with the A.R.P., Mrs Burnett worked in Millbay Laundry, and sometimes she would darn Servicemen's socks. Often she worked a twelve-hour shift, went home for a quick tea, donned her steel helmet and then went into the streets for her A.R.P. duties.

~ *BOARDING A BUS AT ST ANDREW'S CROSS* ~

The photograph of passengers boarding a coach was taken at St Andrew's Cross, a favourite rendezvous for everyone before the war (like Derry's Clock). Mrs B. Hunt recollected that this was the starting point for Western National buses and she thought that the picture was taken about 1935, which it was.

Mrs Hunt remembered it well because it was from there that she caught coaches for family outings to places like Noss Mayo and Wembury. And the queues? 'Well, they were not orderly,' she commented, somewhat surprisingly.

Passengers climb aboard a bus at St Andrew's.

Mr F.G. Frampton pointed out that this terminus was just above the magistrates' court of the time. And another reader, Joe Pengelly, observed that the upper floors of Spooners department store can be seen in the background.

~ *TALES OF SOLOMON'S WISDOM* ~

Solomon Stephens was on Plymouth Town (later City) Council for a record-breaking forty-five years, a unique link between the late Victorian era and the rebuilding of Plymouth after the Blitz. He helped to make important decisions about Plymouth's development from 1902 onwards, and was an enthusiastic supporter of the post-war rebuilding plans.

The photograph shows him in his role as Lord Mayor, officially closing the toll booth at Laira Bridge on 1 April 1924. This event was well remembered

Mayor Solomon Stephens, cuts the tape to free Laira Bridge from its toll in 1924.

by Mrs Dorothea Ladyman, who was ninety at the time she wrote to the Herald. She pointed out that the mace-bearer at the end, on the right-hand side of the picture, was a relative, Mr Abraham Farmer.

The toll to cross Laira Bridge (known as the Iron Bridge) was much disliked by all Plymothians. When it was abolished, along with the other three tolls, in 1924, a local ditty was sung:

> Now we pay no longer, from today it's free;
> No more will you pay for the pleasure of walking over me.
> I should have been 'done in' five score years ago,
> For a town the size of Plymouth my finish has been slow.

Solomon Stephens, twice Mayor of Plymouth, was a great pre-war Liberal Party figure. Hugh Caldwell observed that he was a member of the local council from 1902 to 1946 and that he dominated pre-war Liberal politics. He stood unsuccessfully against the Conservative magnate Sir Arthur Shirley Benn at one general election. When he went on the inaugural flight from Plymouth to Belfast in 1924, he was so thrown about by the bumpy flight that he emerged the other end badly bruised and shaken.

Mr Caldwell, who lived in Plymouth for eighty years, recalled that when Solomon Stephens died in 1950, at the age of eighty-six, he had opened seventeen Stephens bakery shops and three bakehouses. His six daughters each ran one of the shops.

~ *WHEN FRIENDSHIP KNEW NO PARTY LINES* ~

When Leslie Paul was elected to the old Vintry ward of the City Council in 1936, Plymouth's northern boundaries stopped at Higher Compton Road; Crownhill was incorporated two years later, almost doubling the city's acreage. The city had been granted a Lord Mayoralty status just the previous year and Roborough airport had been opened by the Prince of Wales in 1931.

Mr Paul had first tried to get on the council in 1935, at Valletort, losing by only twenty-three votes against a strong Labour victor. 'I made my name at that one,' he said simply. 'It was a tough Labour stronghold, so to come so close to winning did not go unnoticed.'

Vintry covered the Barbican area and wound up to Sherwell. Mr Paul was soon introduced into the singular Barbican crowd and it wasn't long before he got caught up in the big municipal issue of the day: should cinemas open on Sundays?

'The debate was passionate, as so many were in those days. One councillor flourished a Bible and told us that we would be breaking God's commandments if we opted for opening. There were fierce charges and countercharges, and eventually the Sabbatarians won the day.' But he said that the Government ordered them to open on Sundays anyway in 1940, 'and that proves that we were right all along'.

Leslie F. Paul, former Lord Mayor and leader of the Conservative group on Plymouth City Council.

Names of some of the council giants of those days rolled off Mr Paul's tongue – Lovell Dunstan, Solomon Stephens, George Scoble, Harry Mason, Harry Wright, Bert Medland, Clifford Tozer and, of course, Lord and Lady Astor. 'We had orators in their own right on council. If we were having a smoke in the corridor of the old municipal building and we heard that one of them was about to speak, we would rush into the chamber.'

Mr Paul recalled the high level of goodwill that existed over party lines. 'After a council meeting, a few of us from the Conservative side would go over to the Lounge pub at Stoke and swop yarns with the Labour people. There was a good deal of leg-pull and laughter because we all got on well together, regardless of party.'

He was decidedly in favour of the old system under which the governing party took the chair of a committee, with a member of the opposition as his or her deputy. 'It worked well because our main concern was the welfare of Plymouth. It meant, too, that when the other side got in their councillors had experience of wielding power and working with officers, whereas now they would have to start from scratch.'

Mr Paul represented Vintry until he was called up to the army in 1942, and he had the unique distinction of fighting the 1945 election from Ceylon. His wife, Olive, did what she could but, inevitably, he lost. However, he was back the following year for Vintry. This amalgamated with Sutton to form a Sutton ward and he was invited to fight a by-election at Compton in 1949 which he won.

He was made Lord Mayor in 1957, having served as deputy four years before. For twenty-one years he was to be the central and oft-times stormy figure in local educational circles. He became chairman of the education committee in 1951 and in succeeding years was the automatic Conservative nominee for the chair, or vice-chair, according to which party was in control. A vigorous critic of comprehensive education, his pronouncements on this thorny subject frequently made the headlines.

At 91, he was still working in the family business, the wholesale newsagents Louis F. Paul Ltd, founded by his father in 1894. In 1972 he was made a Freeman of the city and, whatever their politics, few would deny that this controversial man, who was never afraid to stand for unpopular causes, rightly deserved it.

~ THE GREAT DAYS OF WIDEY COURT ~

The sheer joy and exhilaration of living at the old Widey Court permeated readers' letters sent in response to the photograph. Two readers related, most movingly, the pleasure of living in such glorious surroundings, now no longer in existence. For Widey Court was torn down after the war because it had been allowed to sink into such a state of disrepair – a familiar enough story in Plymouth, unfortunately.

Pleas for it to be retained and used as a unique Civil War centre fell on deaf ears. So Widey Court joined the long list of stately homes in Plymouth which fell victim, not to Nazi bombs, but to the Corporation's demolition squads. All the correspondents bemoaned the destruction of the fine old building.

Mrs Pamela Magill pointed out that the present Widey Court Primary School stands on the hallowed site. 'Widey dates back to the Domesday Book days and gets its name from the withy beds that used to be there. Its main claim to fame is that Charles I stayed there during the Civil War, issuing a proclamation for Plymouth to surrender to him.

'My particular interest is because my grandfather, Sergeant Benjamin Frowde, lived there with his wife, Margaret, and their ten children during the war. And my father and mother, Ernest and Lilia Frowde, had their wedding reception there in March 1945.

'My aunts speak of grand staircases, ballrooms and the "King Charles" bedroom which used to have an effigy of Charles on the bed, stables, beautiful gardens and oak panelling everywhere.'

Mrs Audrey Thurlow had the joy of living in the old place for over four years during the war because her father was given the job of police caretaker there. She recollected that it was taken over for police accommodation during the war, should the Greenbank station be put out of action – which, in fact, happened only once.

'There were bunk beds in readiness and Widey Grange was taken over to be used as a telephone exchange, the ground floor being reinforced with girders,' she remembered. 'We had the benefit of a lovely garden, with grapes and peaches growing up the wall.

'The grassy bank leading from the Lodge to the big house was always a blaze of colour during the spring, with crocus. It was a lovely place in which to live. And weren't we lucky when it snowed because we tobogganed down the field to the walnut tree at the bottom. The room next to my bedroom was where King Charles was supposed to have slept; it was quite creepy!'

Mrs Thurlow recalled that the Lodge, at the end of the main drive, was occupied by a Mrs Fitzgerald, who was awarded the George Cross for driving ambulances during the Blitz.

Widey Court, one of Plymouth's vanished stately homes.

Another lady with personal recollections of Widey was Mrs Barbara Erwaker, who said she spent the happiest times in her life there. She was children's nanny to the 'delightful daughters' of Commander and Mrs Millington, who used to live there.

'On the day war was declared we were picking blackberries and my tears mingled with the fruit. We used to play in all the secret little places. Many of the nannies in Crownhill used to come to tea and enjoyed the lovely old place as much as we did.' Mrs Erwaker also remembered a lovely old four-poster in one wing of the house, plus an impressive ballroom. 'Now it's all no more; such a sad thing to have seen it in ruins!'

~ *DRAKE CIRCUS IN THE 1950s* ~

Many readers recognised Drake Circus in the early 1950s, before it was all swept out of the way for the new city centre. One reader even thought that she could see her car in one of the pictures!

The photographs reminded Reg Heggie of a hilarious incident when he went into an office in the area to get insured before travelling to Iraq in 1952. 'The assistant looked up and said "Could you tell me where the wreck is, please?" It took me several seconds to get her to realise I had said Iraq, not "the wreck", and then we had a jolly good laugh together.'

Referring to the lower picture, Mr Heggie observed: 'The old technical college can be seen in the top middle of the picture. The corner of the Austin Showrooms is also visible, with J. and M. Stone on the left-hand side and the temporary single-storey Spooners shop on the right.'

Joe McCarthy recognised the premises named by Mr Heggie, but added that the British School of Motoring occupied the building shown on the right

This view is taken from the corner of Park Street and Tavistock Road, looking south to the junction of Ebrington Street with Old Town Street.

53

of centre, between the two buses. He also mentioned that the Spooners shop
was one of many scattered around the city pending the development of their
permanent department store in Royal Parade.

K.R. Algar pointed out that the Midland Bank was next door. Meanwhile,
an anonymous correspondent named some of the types of cars seen in the
photos, including a Hillman Minx, an Opel Rekord, a Vauxhall and various
Ford models. This reader also identified the old post office at the northern
end of the Drake Circus block. The city museum was just out of sight on the
right-hand side of the lower picture.

Suzanne Sainsbury recalled that her sister, Liz Waggett, was apprenticed to
Maison Terry, seen in the picture, while she herself was on a secretarial
course at the technical school opposite. Then she added: 'I'm sure that's my
Austin 8 parked just down from the post office! We had to leave it on the
downward slope because the battery was flat and the brakes were inade-
quate.'

The area was a familiar one to Jeanne Curle. She was born above
Chapman's motor showrooms, which belonged to her father, in Old Town
Street.

Out of view, of course, is the famous Guinness clock. This dominated the
scene for many years until it was pulled down to make way for the advance
of the new city centre.

~ THE GLOBE THEATRE ~

Many a Plymothian has heard the steady clip-clop of high heels echoing
under a moonlit sky on the expanse of the Royal Marine Barracks in
Durnford Street. The sound would be coming from people leaving a show at
that compact and delightfully intimate little gem, the Globe Theatre.

Several readers who had performed there wrote in to recall their memories, and all regretted its closure, for security reasons, at the turn of the last decade. Patrick Hodge pointed out that it was built as a racquets court in 1788. Not long afterwards it became a theatre and it was extensively improved in the early nineteenth century.

The stage of the Globe Theatre.

'It was considered one of the finest and best-maintained small Regency theatres in the country,' he recalled. 'The Little Mermaid, Coward's Corner, King Oggie of Guzz, Inherit the Wind, A Voyage Round My Father, a Battle of Britain concert and even a local Mr Universe contest are among my personal memories of the old place – small, but cosy.

'Such groups as the Rapier Company, the Shakespeare Society, the Carmenians and the Gilbert and Sullivan Fellowship, among others, often played at the Globe.'

Marian Matthews did many shows there in her younger days with the Bedford Academy, before the troupe's panto at the Palace. 'We all had to be over eleven. I recall happy days. I wish I could turn the clock back for a while; simple things, lots to do, never bored, not much money, but happy.'

When she was a nurse at the Scott Hospital, Mrs Jean Pattison used to help put on pantomimes at the Globe. 'It was a lovely little theatre ideally suited for shows, and we received every assistance from the Marines based there. We were very disappointed when it was closed for security reasons as nowhere else could we find such an ideal place. Everything was there – stalls, circle and dressing rooms under the stage, where you could walk off one side, cross underneath and appear on the other.'

Mrs Dorothy Calton also trod the theatre's boards when she was a member of the Royal Marines Girls Ambulance Company. 'We did a display of First Aid and then a pantomime. The Royal Marine Boys Cadets showed their skills with a P.T. display, covering the ages eleven to fourteen. My last performance on its stage was in December 1936,' she remembered.

Suzanne Sainsbury performed as a dancer and a pianist at the Globe, as well as watching many productions there. 'The last one I saw before the security precautions was Salad Days,' she said. Another reader, Reg Heggie, recalled that his last visit there was to see the Dockyard Revue Company put on Aladdin; his daughter was in the chorus. All the correspondents expressed their hope that the Globe would one day open again.

~ PRYOR'S ACADEMY ~

With the death of Miss Kay Pryor, at the age of seventy-nine, in 1981, a unique feature of old Plymouth came to an end. Although an outstanding city councillor, her name is inextricably bound to Pryor's Academy which was founded by her uncle in 1887 and which she ran after the death of her mother in 1938.

Originally in Westwell Street, it was later based in the Peverell Park Assembly Rooms (off Weston Park Road) and later moved to Queen Anne Terrace, before going in with the Warran School, on North Hill. Miss Pryor, a woman of real zest and drive, was awarded the M.B.E. in 1959 for her political and public services, in particular for education and the welfare of the elderly. She was a woman of gracious and dignified presence, according to Miss Muriel Newman, former headmistress of Plymouth High School, of which she was chairman of the Board of Governors.

Many readers studied shorthand and typing at one or other of Pryor's different sites and were keen to share their memories. Miss Minnie Grainger was one of several who pointed out that, at one stage, Pryor's Academy was situated halfway down the former Westwell Street. She went there in 1935 and recalled that 'all the young ladies were obliged to wear hats when attending. Sometimes Miss Pryor used to start dictating as soon as she entered the room, before we were even ready with our notebooks. On one occasion, during a bus strike, she drove me home to Milton Combe.'

Mrs S.M. Gaydon attended the Academy for a year in the 1960s, after it had moved from Queen Anne's Terrace, when Miss Whitfield was headteacher. She took the pupils in typing. 'I thoroughly enjoyed my time there. I do remember Miss Whitfield being strict, but it paid off with good results,' she recalled. 'The discipline was just like school, but being an ex-Devonport High School girl I knew all about strict discipline. At Pryor's we were certainly expected to behave in a ladylike manner!'

Mrs Gaydon added: 'The typewriters we used were antiquated, mostly old Imperials. The keys were round with metal rings around them. One really had to thump them to make an imprint – a bit different from today's word processing.'

The former Pryor's Academy in North Hill.

Another former pupil was Mrs Pauline Dulley, who attended when the Academy was in Peverell. As a fourteen-year-old, straight from school, she remembered Miss Pryor as 'quite a formidable lady' who dictated to those students who had acquired a high shorthand speed. 'After less than a year I obtained certificates in shorthand and typing and a job as a shorthand typist with a well-known firm of building contractors. The skills I learned at Pryor's enabled me to continue my career for forty-five years.'

Mrs Eileen Ross was a pupil at Pryor's during the 1930s, after leaving Plymouth High School. That was in its Westwell Street days. Apparently, it was rather a run-down property, almost next to the General Post Office and flanked on its other side by two very convenient shops – Solomon Stephens the baker's and The Three Towns Dairy.

'At that time Miss Pryor's mother was in charge or, should I say, was a dominant figure who sat in the office overseeing the general running of the establishment,' she remembered. 'The typewriters were housed in a sort of glassed-in corridor at the back of the building where we had excellent tuition from, amongst others, Miss Pryor, Miss Whitford and Miss Pile. A dear old chap named Mr Spry maintained the typewriters.'

Mrs Ross, or Miss Gulley as she then was, later joined the staff, remaining for three or four years before taking the Civil Service exam, and then moving to the G.P.O. in the same street. She commented that the concentrated tuition of touch-typing and high-speed shorthand meant that 'a pupil at Pryor's Academy in those days was assured of employment'.

Another reader who recalled the strict discipline was Mrs L.R. Lancaster, who also remarked that during the war Miss Pryor ran her school at a garage showroom in Western Park Road. 'I attended there at the age of fifteen, in 1943, to do a shorthand-typing course. Having done very well, I was employed by the solicitor Mr W.H. Sloman, in Athenaeum Street, until my marriage in 1952. Such happy days!'

The most up-to-date memories came from Mrs Deirdre Sears who remembered Pryor's Academy when it was on the first floor of Warran School, North Hill, where she was educated. 'As we attended our classes in our neat uniforms I can remember being envious of the girls at Pryor's who at that time wore whatever they liked! When I finished school I went on to study at the Academy. I can't remember the staff but I vividly recall all the different typewriters. We had to use them in turn so that when we got jobs we would understand any of them. There was one which must have been an antique even in 1946. School days were so happy and the discipline didn't do us any harm at all,' she added, echoing the views of so many former pupils.

~ DAYS OF THE SILVER SCREEN ~

It was cosy, it was small and the staff were friendly but firm. That's how readers remembered the Belgrave cinema, shown in the photograph.

Mr J. James worked there as a doorman for several years. His late wife was one of the usherettes and a Mrs Doris Evans the other. The commissionaire was Mr Walter Hirons. The management had their own way of dealing with the noisy mob in those days! 'They were warned to behave and, if they still did not do so, were turfed out and would be barred from coming to the cinema again until we thought they had learned their lesson.'

Mr Ken Gardiner had memories of the Belgrave stretching back to 1932, when he went there as a young schoolboy. He recalled that, in those days, there were two types of certification – A and B. If it was the former, youngsters under sixteen weren't allowed to buy their own tickets, and the trick was to be 'adopted' by an adult patron, or even a passer-by.

'It meant anyone approaching the Belgrave who looked over sixteen would be besieged by children and asked to take us in, whether or not it was their intention to go to the cinema. This often resulted in a mad scramble by the children because adults could buy only two tickets for an under-sixteen. That person would be responsible for your behaviour throughout the whole performance.'

The old Belgrave cinema.

Mr Gardiner also remembered that, during the showing of the films, there used to be 'a lot of bouncing up and down on the seats, booing and hissing against the "baddies" and deafening cheers for the "goodies". At the end of the performance we filed out of the cinema with the noises still echoing in our ears.'

Mr A.C. Lee said that he and three pals used to book regularly for the Saturday evening show, at nine old pennies each. He commented that the outstanding personality was the commissionaire, always resplendent and immaculate in his braided uniform. 'He was a very genial but "no-nonsense" man.'

The cinema opened at about 6.30 p.m., he recalled, and 'we would applaud when the orchestra put in an appearance because we knew the show was about to start. First it was the Pathe Gazette news, followed by a feature film. How the musicians worked to depict the various moods of the story unfolding before us! During the thirty-minute interval we would leave the cinema and visit the tuck shop in the adjacent lane.

'The second half of the show would sometimes start with a popular song played by the orchestra, with words shown on the screen. So we had a singsong, followed by a second film.' The show always finished with the National Anthem when the audience stood perfectly still.

Alderman W. Ivor Thompson recalled that the proprietor, John Prance, was 'a friendly man, anxious to make his patrons feel at home. He and his few staff showed you, with the aid of a torch, to your seat. If you had missed seeing a film at one of the major cinemas you had another chance at the Belgrave.'

Mr Thompson, Lord Mayor in 1975–6, heard in recent years that Mr Prance had died in Australia, where he emigrated some years ago.

~ THE OLD OPORTO PUB ~

The Oporto pub had something in common with the Belgrave cinema – both establishments carved a warm niche in the hearts of many Plymothians, who will never forget either.

Someone with personal memories of the Oporto was W.G. Baker, whose relatives, Flo and Fred Parker, ran the pub when it opened in the mid 1930s. It was built for Messrs Popplestones at the junction of York Street and Cobourg Lane.

Another personal touch was provided by Mr R.W. Gotham, who remembered his father helping to build the Oporto. He lived opposite, at 24 York Street, and helped to put down the crazy paving slabs in the front. 'It was funny to see the picture of workmen taking its roof off when I saw them putting it on all those years ago,' he reflected. 'I was courting my future wife at the time and we enjoyed many good occasions in that pub. When it closed all the patrons came out, stood around and sang "When they sound the last All Clear, oh, how happy they would be".'

Ken Headon had another, very important memory of the Oporto, for he and his wife, with the best man, popped in for a few drinks just after they had got married at the nearby Registry Office in Belle Vue Place. 'I'll never forget the occasion,' he said.

Mrs Doreen Collister was another reader who lived opposite the pub, above Pooley's bakery shop. She described the other local premises: 'Next door was a sweet shop run by a mother and her daughter and, at the top end of York Street, two other public houses, called the Albion and the Mewtower. A little further down from the Oporto was a furniture store called Baudains.'

~ *THE HEART OF THE OLD CITY* ~

Pictures of old Plymouth, as well as stirring up memories of old buildings, also arouse feelings of nostalgia for the old city's ethos. Referring to the period when this photo was taken, one writer said that Plymouth then was well-policed. 'Everybody knew everybody else. We could all walk safely where we liked at any time of day or night – and we did.' There was a comparative tranquillity, it seems, very much at variance with the present aggressive, sometimes violent, city.

Mr B. LeBearn was one of a number of readers who provided details of this city centre scene. He pointed out that St Andrew's Church can be seen sitting grandly in the centre foreground, as it had for centuries, with the cross standing in its little garden. At the base of the cross was a tablet commemorating The Shambles (or meat market) that once stood on the site.

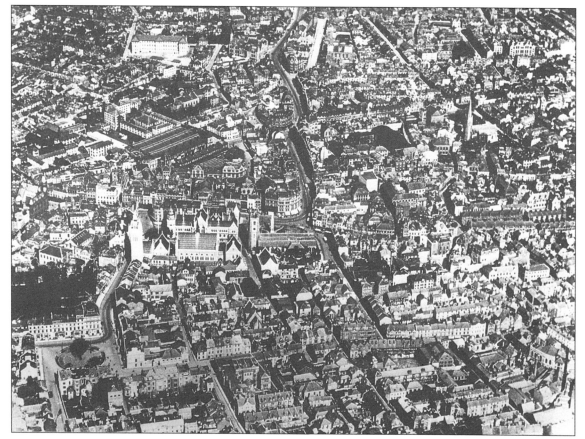

The Guildhall Square, then the main site for outdoor public gatherings, is seen in the centre, next to the city treasury and Catherine Street. The General Post Office is clearly visible at the centre top, fronting on to Westwell Street, which sported several shops, including the fishmongers Churchill's. 'Then you came to that quiet, tree-lined haven of Westwell Gardens, a one-time extension graveyard for St Andrew's. This road led into Princess Square, on the corner of which stood the Repertory Theatre.'

Mr LeBearn pointed out that westbound traffic used either Basket Street or Bedford Street, next to Bateman's Corner; the former accommodated three tram tracks and pavements only two feet wide, and just two feet from the trams at that! George Baker remembered that top-deck tram passsengers passing through Basket Street could 'shake hands across the narrow gap'.

He recalled those wonderful times 'when financial circumstances allowed the purchase of a milk shake from the milk-bar in Basket Street – the first of its kind in Plymouth – at four old pennies a glass'.

Along with these two correspondents, Don Chapman identified Spooners' corner at the bottom right of the picture. He remembered the 'happy sing-songs at the Guildhall Square on New Year's Eve'.

This shot, taken in 1939 clearly shows some of the main shopping streets in the old city centre.

Another reader, Tony Foale, remembered his grandfather buying him a 7s. 6d. (now 37.5p) 'Star' yacht in the Swiss toy shop in Old Town Street, in the heart of old Plymouth.

~ *POUND STREET SHOPS* ~

This photograph evoked memories for Mr William Tapper, for he was born at what was then 1 Compton Street, just behind the Harvest Home. The public house can be seen here at the end of Pound Street, at one end of which was Tavistock Road and at the other Cobourg Street.

Mr Tapper went to school at the nearby Ebenezer Hall, later known as the Central Hall, rented out to the council for such purposes. 'My maternal great-grandmother lived in Saltash Street, above a confectioners shop until she was in her nineties,' he recalled.

Mrs E. Martin was another reader who had a close connection with this area. She worked in Harvey's, the butcher's shop, where they made pasties and sold cooked legs of pork. 'I was manageress and loved every minute of the work,' she said, remembering also that a small sweet shop, a cafe and a school clinic were in the area.

Many people, of course, remembered the Harvest Home pub. It was once a staging post, Jeanne Curle pointed out. 'The shops further down on the left, just past the junction with Saltash Street, included Millbay Laundry, Avery Scales and a pork butchers famous for its sausages.'

A view of Pound Street just after the Second World War.

Mrs Marian Hutchings could even recall one of the hoardings in Pound Street – it dealt with vivisection. Meanwhile, Mr Thomas Taylor observed that the old technical school stood behind those hoardings and that this 'building of quality' would have been over a hundred years old now had it not been demolished after the war. Noticing the bus in the picture, Mr F.G. Frampton commented that the return fare to Torquay in those days was a mere five shillings.

ST ANDREW'S CHURCH RISES FROM THE ASHES

January 15, 1949 was a red-letter day in Plymouth's post-war recovery, for it marked the rebuilding of the shattered St Andrew's Church, largely destroyed in the Blitz eight years earlier.

Princess Elizabeth (now the Queen) leaves in the rain after the ceremony marking the beginning of the restoration of St. Andrew's Church.

Nine months later Princess Elizabeth, then twenty-three, came to the city and laid the stone commemorating the beginning of the church's restoration, completed in 1957.

Mrs Hazel Boscawen remembered the sense of elation which gripped the city during the young Princess's visit – repeated when, as Queen Elizabeth, she visited during her jubilee year in 1977. Mrs Boscawen recalled: 'Even those of us who weren't Anglicans were elated to see tangible evidence of the notice "Resurgam" (I will rise again) fixed over the north door the day after the Blitz.'

A feature of particular interest in the restored church is the central east window, dedicated to the memory of Lady Astor (in fact, a Christian Scientist!), who was a Plymouth M.P. from 1919 to 1945. The tower window was given in memory of her husband, Waldorf, 2nd Viscount Astor, who preceded his wife in the Plymouth Sutton seat. The Astors were also, of course, Lord Mayor and Lady Mayoress from 1939 to 1944.

~ *WESLEY METHODIST CHURCH* ~

The photograph shows Wesley Methodist Church, in Millbay Road, under construction. It was built to replace the old King Street Church which was destroyed in the Blitz.

Wesley Methodist Church, on the edge of the city centre, under construction.

Mrs Suzanne Sainsbury remembered King Street Church: she was married there. She also said that she had worshipped in the bombed ruins with her godfather, Eugene de jersey Robin, who was a local preacher, manager of Lloyd's Bank, Stonehouse, and an evacuee from the Channel Islands.

Michael Chown, a regular worshipper at Wesley Methodist Church, recognised the building under construction. Next to it is Wesley Hall. The premises were opened on 4 December 1957 by Miss Mabel Almond. 'She could not have unlocked the front door with the key, even if she had wanted to, because there was no lock on that door!' Mr Chown recalled. 'I was thankful to be present even though I was doing my National Service at the time.'

Mr Robertson went back a little further: he remembered that, before the Blitz, the present site of the church was partly occupied by Cooks the travel agents.

~ *A RECONSTRUCTION SCENE* ~

The photograph shows Russell Street, looking towards York Street, in the early days of post-war reconstruction.

It revived memories of a 'thick ear' for John Woodrow. 'When Wakehams went bankrupt a few of us went to the Oporto, at the top of York Street, for a pint and then off home for a thick ear from mother who had never heard the word bankrupt before!'

An early reconstruction scene in the city centre.

Stella Tucker remembered taking her Sunday dinner to Goodbody's bakery, in the adjacent Mill Street, to be cooked when her gas at home was knocked out of action – and it only cost her sixpence!

William Jackson identified the white-tiled building at the junction with York Street as a Plymouth Co-op funeral parlour.

~ V.E. DAY PARADE ~

Plymouth people love a band, and none more than a Royal Marines band. This was certainly the case on V.E. Day, 8 May 1945, when this photograph was taken.

Joan Rickard was one of the nurses in the picture – on the extreme left, just behind the front nurse. She thought that her father, the late Alderman H.J. Perry, was on the dais on the extreme left of the shot, wearing the deputy Lord Mayor's robes, with, possibly, his wife in front.

'I felt very honoured to be able to take part in the parade, but it was hard on the feet. I was twenty-one at the time. We started in Beaumont Road, St Jude's, walked down through the town and the whole length of Union Street, finishing at Stonehouse. The music from the bands certainly helped us along!'

Further information came from Mr Ted Savage, who was serving in the Far East as a musician on H.M.S. London at the time. (He also saw action on the Ajax in the Battle of the River Plate in 1939.) He identified the band as the R.M.'s from the Royal Naval School of Music, from Scarborough, marching

Led by a Royal Marines band, this parade was to celebrate V.E. Day.

down Bedford Street, with Whimple Street in the rear and St Andrew's Church on their left. They are saluting the Lord Mayor of the time, Alderman Harry Mason.

In the left foreground are the colours of the R.M. Old Comrades' Association, various youth groups and a contingent of young local nurses, most of whom, unbelievably, would now be in their middle to late seventies.

SMALL WAS BEAUTIFUL IN POST-WAR HOUSING

They may have looked like squat little boxes, but they were lovely to live in. That was the unanimous verdict of Herald readers on the prefab homes shown in the photograph below. Thousands of these houses were hurriedly erected by the 'get-up-and-go' city council of those days, to house the large numbers who had been made homeless during the Second World War.

The measure was intended to be a temporary one but stretched into years, the way these things do. No one minded, however: indeed, some readers called for the return of these houses to help ease the current chronic housing shortage.

'My parents lived in one for many years at King's Tamerton and loved every moment of it,' wrote one reader. Others described them as smashing, heavenly, comfortable, roomy – anything but what they actually looked like.

Some of the city's first post-war prefab homes.

67

Mrs Jenny Hill could even remember them when she was coming up for three, in 1947. She was taken to the bottom of Nicholson Road, Crownhill, where finishing touches were being put to the new prefabs. 'We were so happy to have a lovely new place in which to live. They were smashing little places. There were two bedrooms, a bathroom (no more tin bath for us!), a lounge-diner and a fitted kitchen which even had a small built-in fridge. Mum made us ice blocks out of the baby's orange juice.'

She recalled that German prisoners of war were still building the road outside the house and would dig a plot in the garden. 'Our grateful mum would give them five Woodbines.'

A similar note was struck by June Luxton, who observed that, although they were boxy, the prefabs were very comfortable and had a coal fire with doors in the grate. She moved into No. 7 St Peter's Road just before her third birthday, and remained there until she was sixteen. 'Then we knew what friendship was! Everyone knew everyone and you weren't afraid to leave your door unlocked because we were all like one big happy family. I was ill for a long time and everyone mucked in to take care of me.'

Someone else who lived in St Peter's Road was Mrs T. Taylor, who had her first home in one of the prefabs. She remembered some of the neighbours' names – Healey, Palmer, Hunter, Goss, Spry and Paramore.

Another reader recalled that there was a community of prefab houses at Millbridge on the site of the old naval hospital tennis courts, with another at the nearby King's Road. The residents used to register their ration books at Lipton's and they used to bring the rebates from their gas meters for her to change, she said. Sometimes this was as much as the equivalent of 50p, a tidy sum fifty years ago.

Reg Heggie recollected that the prefabs were made by the Americans and bought by Plymouth City Council in large numbers. 'The prefabs were complemented by a great number of Swedish-style prefabs which were also bought. They all had an estimated life-span of ten years, but we all know that some thirty years later they were still being used.'

The other photograph shows a row of prefab shops, also put up after the war. Various locations for this picture were suggested by Herald readers. One suggested the north side of Princess Square at the bottom of Windsor Square, facing other premises in Westwell Street. Another opted for Glanville Street, which ran from James Street to Tavistock Road, opposite the library.

Betty Barnes, on the other hand, thought that they were in Tavistock Road, opposite the public library. She was probably right because she went on to recount how, in March 1950, her future husband had a suit made at the Fifty-Shilling Tailors then occupying one of the Nissen huts. In those days you had to order a suit three months in advance, apparently, but this system nearly broke down, to Mrs Barnes' great consternation.

'I went to fetch it two weeks before the wedding – he was away – and it hadn't arrived,' she recalled. 'Deliveries were once a week, so I went to collect the suit the following week and it still hadn't arrived. I was very upset; the wedding was on the following Saturday. They tried to trace it, but no luck. So they suggested we choose one of the "mis-fits" off the peg.

'I didn't see the suit until I arrived at the church. I couldn't help laughing when I saw my future husband. He looked like a "wide boy" in a dark grey suit with wide white stripes – it was horrible! We still laugh about it and, yes, eventually we did get the suit we ordered.'

Mr G. Baker remembered Wright's the chemists, occupying one of the prefabs. 'They were one of the few shops where you could buy films and have them developed; black and white – there were no colour films in those days.'

CELEBRATING THE ESCAPE OF THE AMETHYST

The photograph records the civic reception held to honour the sailors from H.M.S. *Amethyst* after her daring dash down the Yangtse River to evade the Chinese in 1949.

It was an event that held the country spellbound and Plymothians turned out in their thousands to welcome home the brave boys as they marched proudly down the newly cut Royal Parade on 1 November. Hundreds of small boats went out into the harbour to greet the vessel and her company was given a tumultuous welcome.

At the reception, Drake's Drum was on display (seen on the 'Jack flag' in the photograph) – a memento of another daring sailor and on loan from Buckland Abbey.

The civic reception honouring the crew of H.M.S. *Amethyst*.

An interesting response to this picture was received from Enid Ware. She had been in Hong Kong at the time that the *Amethyst* was in port before sailing home. 'They gave a marvellous party for the children of Service families. All the crew dressed as pirates. The kids had to go below and drink dragon's blood and have a skull and crossbones rubber-stamped on their hands.

'When we got home in 1954 – after being rescued from the Empire Windrush which caught fire in the Mediterranean – I was allocated a prefab in Crownhill Road, opposite St Budeaux parish church.' Mrs Ware was as enthusiastic about her prefab home as the readers quoted earlier.

Mr G. Baker remembered that after the *Amethyst* returned to Plymouth she was used to make the film Yangtse Incident, starring Richard Todd. Her final resting place, where she was broken up, was the slipway and breakers' yard in Sutton Road, close to the China House.

~ *A DAY OF PRIDE* ~

The bands played, the flags flew and the servicemen and women from Britain, the Commonwealth and the U.S.A. marched with erect shoulders and pride on their faces – as well they might. It was August 1945 and Plymothians turned out in their thousands to celebrate V.J. Day in a dazzling display.

The route was the former Bedford Street, once a main shopping thoroughfare and on the main bus route into Old Town Street. The shattered remains

Nurses leading a parade to celebrate V.J. Day.

of the municipal offices stand gaunt and open on the right. Sailors from the Free French Navy are in the crowd which was bathed in glorious sunshine.

A reader from Stonehouse was able to identify one of the marchers as former children's nurse Joan Rickard, whose story was told in that stunning home-grown production High Heels in the Rubble, performed at the Theatre Royal in 1991. (See also 'V.E. Day parade' on p. 66.)

~ F.A. CUP MATCH AT HOME PARK ~

Nearly 40,000 heaving, happy Argyle fans were packed into Home Park to watch their favourites match their skills against one of the top sides of the day – Wolverhampton Wanderers. The season was 1950–51 and it was the third round of the F.A. Cup. Wolves were the holders and won 2–1.

Robert Hicks, the sports-minded M.P. for South-east Cornwall, had no trouble in identifying the photograph. He recalled: 'The previous season Argyle had also drawn Wolves at home in the third round. They drew 1–1, with Argyle's left-winger, Williams, scoring. Argyle lost the replay 3–0. I was there on both occasions.'

Harley Lawer's excellent book Argyle Classics lists the Wolves team which played in both games as: Williams, McClean, Pritchard, Crook, Chatham, Wright, Hancocks, Swinbourne, Pye, Smythe and Mullen. The Argyle team was: Short, Ratcliffe, Jones, Douglas, Chisholm, McShane, Strauss, Squires, Tadman, Dews and Williams.

Mr G. Waterfield remembered that the cup was put on display in the window of the Herald offices in Frankfort Street for three days, drawing crowds of adoring worshippers. 'A junior clerk and myself took the cup by taxi to the offices at 10 a.m. and collected it again at 4 p.m., returning it to the strong room of the National Provincial Bank. My manager had his photograph taken holding the cup in his office. I took it outside and took a photograph of it but – bad luck! – the film didn't come out,' he added.

The F.A. Cup being displayed at Home Park when Plymouth Argyle played Wolves in a cup match in 1951.

One of the members of the St John Ambulance Brigade when Wolves came down for the cup was Mr L.M. Coville. 'I remember helping to secure the cup on one of our stretchers prior to it being taken around the ground, and that was before the grandstand was rebuilt.' He also recalled that Leo Chalkley, who has since died, was one of the stretcher-carriers on that auspicious occasion, and Les Kiver another.

I can also remember watching the Argyle replay with Wolves at Molineaux in 1949. I was just a young lad then, stationed in nearby Castle Bromwich, Birmingham. Although suitably chastened by the fact that Wolves rammed in three goals without reply, I remember being blessed to bits by the generosity and good humour of the Wolves crowd towards the defeated team. But that's how it was in those days.

~ A MUCH-LOVED COLLEGE ~

They called it the Plymouth and Devonport Technical and Art College. It was an impressive pile of Victorian buildings in Tavistock Road, almost opposite the city museum and art gallery. The photograph shows part of this institution, before it was demolished in recent years.

A number of readers enjoyed personal associations with the old place, which they clearly held in high esteem. They are sorry that it has gone, particularly since it was replaced by a pile of buildings which look drearily functional and ugly, devoid of any architectural embellishment.

Part of the massive walls of Plymouth and Devonport Technical and Art College.

Roger Hawkins observed that the old college was gutted by the demolition squads in the late 1960s and that the site is now occupied by security offices. Queen Anne Terrace, looking very much as it does today, is on the opposite side of the street, and just up from the college, behind the shops, the spire of Sherwell Church is pointing to the sky.

Mrs E. Fedrick was pleased to see once again one of the city's beautiful old buildings 'after the concrete jungle we live in today, I quite agree with Prince Charles about modern architecture!' She pointed out that the young lady in the picture would be crossing over to the Harvest Home at the beginning of Cobourg Street, and added that the tram lines were coming up from Drake Circus. Mr Hawkins also had some interesting comments to make on the tram lines which, he recalled, were part of the final route between Peverell Corner and the centre, then called 'Theatre', via Mutley Plain.

A more sobering note is struck by Devonport historian Gerald Barker, who recalled that the names of air-raid casualties were posted to the right of the front door. 'I often walked past the list and, inside, one of the ladies would hand me a list containing the names of people who could not be accounted for after a heavy raid,' he wrote. 'Later, together with other young post-Blitz messenger boys, I would endeavour to find out what had happened to the missing persons.'

Referring to the advertisement, on the corner of Glanville Street and Tavistock Road, for 'Oatmeal Stout' at 2s. 6d. per dozen, Mr S. Robertson pointed out that this was a tenth of the average wage of the time!

D.E. Coleman attended the college from 1943–6, studying for a degree. 'We used to swim on The Hoe most mornings before lectures and go into the Three Towns Dairy opposite the college for coffee and a digestive biscuit.'

Another personal link was provided by Enid Ware, whose father – killed, alas, in the First World War – used to teach there at the college. 'Like the museum and library it was a very fine building, not needing constant repair like the present-day concrete monstrosities!'

~ THE BATTLE TO SAVE WINTER VILLA ~

Six cast-iron columns hold pride of place in the garden at Yelverton of former city council 'battler' Mrs Peggy Radmore. She bought them as a reminder of the vigorous though unsuccessful fight she led, over twenty years ago, to save the Italianate Winter Villa from being razed by the demolition squads.

The fifty-room villa, designed in a medley of classical styles, was the largest in England when it was built. Its long, sea-facing facade of coupled Byzantine columns was one of the most imposing sights along the waterfront. But the Sisters of Nazareth wanted to erect an old people's home in its place, and in this they were successful.

The Winter Villa was built on a prominent piece of land once owned by the Durnford family, passing by marriage to the Edgcumbes. Now it is just another sad photograph tucked away somewhere in the city museum.

The imposing cliff-top
site of Winter Villa,
Stonehouse.

Mrs Radmore vividly remembered the great disappointment she and others felt at the time and still believes that a compromise could have been reached to retain the facade of the lovely old building, particularly since it would have cost only £32,000 to have done so, according to the Victorian Society. 'Still, it was not to be,' she wrote. 'Subsequently, I bought the cast-iron columns, renovated and painted them and they now have pride of place in my garden, providing a delightful backdrop, for instance, for the Medieval Dancers who performed there for charity one June.'

Plymouth City Council had agreed to demolish the pile of stately buildings by a crushing vote of forty to eight on 1 September 1975. In doing so they rejected conservationist appeals, endorsing the plan put forward by the Sisters of Nazareth for the demolition of the villa and the erection of a forty-eight-bed old people's home. The Sisters had owned the building since 1932 and accommodated forty children in an adjacent orphanage, purpose-built in 1971.

The Sisters' case was that the elegance of the vista from the Tamar disguised an interior which was decaying and structurally unsound. It had dry and wet rot, the timber was infested and it was a fire hazard, according to Norman Pengelly, chairman of the council's planning committee at the time. He said that the cost of retaining the facade and incorporating it into a new building would be over £500,000 – and that was over twenty years ago, remember.

~ *ISAAC FOOT, CAMPAIGNER AND PREACHER* ~

A Liberal activist and Methodist local preacher all his adult life, Isaac Foot was also a lover of good books and a witty and charming companion. The

life of this redoubtable West Country figure is a treasure trove of memories for those who knew him and grew to understand him.

Born in Notte Street, he was beaten by Lady Astor for the Plymouth Sutton seat in 1919, coming bottom of the poll, but won South-east Cornwall for the Liberals three years later. He was returned five times in that seat, earning a reputation for persistent casework, as befitted a lawyer of his repute.

In 1946 he was Lord Mayor of his native city, an honour which he dearly valued, though it was in the direct aftermath of the city's most fearful nightmare in the form of the Blitz.

The Foot family, of course, is synonymous with West Country politics, three of the four sons making their mark in the hustings. Owen Davis, related to the family by marriage, had rich memories of the famous dynasty, many of them culled from the days when the family attended the huge Wesley Church in Ebrington Street. This held a congregation of close on a thousand and whenever Isaac Foot preached it was full, he recalled.

'He never forgot his Methodist upbringing and he was a great encouragement to me when I became an accredited local preacher in 1928. He preached without notes, quoting many literary notables and spell-binding the congregation with his wonderful oratory.' Mr Davis added that for years Isaac Foot lived at 1 Lipson Terrace, and would encourage the family to browse through his massive collection of books, later to be housed at his Pencreber home, outside Callington.

~ *A LIBERAL LEGEND* ~

Scorned by the local Tories as 'a little pipsqueak of a fellow', Leslie Hore-Belisha's arrival on the local political scene could scarcely have been less promising. A former chairman of the Oxford Union and an army major in the First World War, he had been sent down to Devonport by Liberal headquarters in 1922.

Arriving alone at the main station, he asked a taxi-driver to take him to the Devonport Liberal office – and was promptly told there wasn't such a place! He was taken, instead, to the offices of the Devon and Cornwall Liberal Federation where the secretary advised him to take the next train home. 'Go back, young man,' he said. 'You will have no chance here.'

They were talking to the wrong man. Hore-Belisha had long learned to stay his ground and fight. In the ten days remaining before the 1922 general election he put some fire in the local Liberal bellies, losing by a margin of

Leslie Hore-Belisha and his wife arriving at the Roborough Airport, by de Havilland Rapide, in the 1930s.

Hore-Belisha, on the left, meeting people in one of Devonport's back streets.

only 2,000 votes against the Conservative member, Sir Clement Kinloch-Cooke, who had been regarded as a dead certainty for the seat.

When, in the following year, another election took place, 'The Major', as the boyish Liberal was by then known, ousted him after a whirlwind campaign. And he was subsequently returned another four times by the Devonport electorate. By the 1931 election, having by then fought and won three times, Hore-Belisha, standing for the first time as a National Liberal, was virtually unassailable. With the highest number of votes he ever secured – 23,459 – he crushed his sole opponent, Labour's Paul Reed, by a majority of close on 14,500.

That was his shining hour; from then it was downhill all the way and with gathering speed. The 1935 election was to be his last win in the constituency which had idolised him. Things went desperately wrong for him in the early days of the Second World War when, as War Minister, he carried the can for a shortage of tanks and was sacked by Chamberlain. The first post-war general election saw a Labour landslide and Hore-Belisha was one its many victims.

The Plymouth count, at the city's art gallery, was delayed until all the vital Service votes had come in from overseas. For Leslie Hore-Belisha, dubbed by a grateful Lloyd George twenty years previously as the 'Star of the West', it was to be total eclipse. He arrived late as usual and Eric Cock, his political agent, remembered that he was on the way upstairs when he met a man coming down. 'Which way in?' asked the former Devonport shining light. 'All you want is the way out,' was the brutal reply.

Michael Foot had stormed to a triumphant victory that had his supporters frantic with joy. He had fought a hard, almost ruthless, campaign against Hore-Belisha whom he denounced as a Judas Iscariot for 'time-serving' in the National Government under Baldwin and Chamberlain. Hore-Belisha left the constituency and the area, never to return, his chagrin and deep disappointment obvious to all.

It seems strange now that he is remembered in a universal if unthinking way because of the pedestrian beacons that bear his name, although he had merely brought to fruition an idea inherited from a previous Minister of Transport. However, one of his constituents, Joe Pengelly, remembered him in quite a different way. He recounted that when Hore-Belisha was visiting Crownhill Barracks as Minister of War he declined an offer to dine in the officers' mess and, instead, took his meal with the men. That was a typical, unrehearsed, incident and probably one by which Hore-Belisha would like to be remembered.

~ A TRUE BLUE-RINSE TORY ~

Alex and Beatrice Leest would never forget the warm May night when they stood on the steps of Plymouth museum after the count for the 1955 general election, barely able to believe their eyes and ears. The huge crowd outside, jostling each other in a good-humoured way, was waiting to hail the expected Devonport victor, Michael Foot, the 'local boy made good'. His political charm and outstanding track record was expected to dash the hopes of Conservative candidate Joan Vickers, who had arrived on the scene three years earlier.

Instead, one of the election's biggest shocks was provided when the blue-rinsed battler from the home counties snatched the 'safe' Labour seat by a mere electoral whisker – 100 votes.

For Alex Leest it was a moment to be savoured for the rest of his life. He was behind the careful pincer movement to bring Joan Vickers to Plymouth, short-circuiting several better-known Tory hopefuls in the process and virtually by-passing the approved short list. The local Conservatives had barely recovered from the traumas of handling the unsuccessful and enigmatic Randolph Churchill at the 1951 general election and were looking for someone of an entirely different ilk for their next tilt at the seat.

Mr Leest, who fought his first local election in 1933, remembered that the name of Baroness Vickers (as she later became) was mentioned casually by a local lady who thought she might fit the bill. 'I had a feeling she would and made arrangements for her to come down to face a far-from-convinced selection committee. Dressed to the nines and wearing her spiky-heeled shoes, she arrived here like a whiff of political eau de cologne. She won them all over, just like that. We didn't think she had much of a chance against someone like Michael Foot, but she was to remain our M.P. for just short of twenty years, and a wonderful job she did too.'

Mrs Leest, chairman of the women's branch of the Devonport Conservative Association for many years, recalled that Joan Vickers and others helped to canvass every house in Devonport over a period of three years. 'She worried away at a problem like a terrier with a bone. She was really a welfare M.P., who encouraged anyone to knock at her door and invited constituents with problems to stay overnight in her London flat. They would then both troop off together the following day to get things sorted out.'

In an interview a few years ago, I talked to Baroness Vickers about her time in Plymouth. She recalled: 'I didn't have a car so I went everywhere by bus. I got to know the crews manning them and chatted with people during the ten-minute breaks on the route. Most of them weren't Conservatives and I got a lot of opinions and ideas which sharpened up my own thinking.'

Joan Vickers, who represented Devonport for nearly twenty years.

Party power-brokers still think it was Joan Vickers' intrepid visits to the homes of her electorate that captured the seat for her. 'Well, yes, I did call on between 18,000 and 20,000 homes and, as I say, without a car,' she agreed. 'And, do you know, I didn't discuss politics with the people? They were amazed. I simply introduced myself as the candidate for Devonport and explained that if I was going to ask for their vote the least I could do was to visit them personally. Many people are afraid to discuss politics with a so-called professional and that's often why they shut their doors in your face.'

Joan Vickers was created Dame of the British Empire in 1964, elevated to the House of Lords ten years later and in 1982 received the Freedom of the City of Plymouth, along with several others, one of whom was Michael Foot. Even after her term as an M.P. had ended, she remained a committed fighter for many causes and continued to take an interest in Plymouth's affairs.

~ A LINE-UP OF M.P.'s ~

The photograph shows three of Plymouth's one-time M.P.s recorded at the 1951 general election. Lucy Middleton gamely held the Sutton seat for Labour, until J.J. Astor, seen next to her with his current wife, took it from her in 1951. Michael Foot retained Devonport against the challenge of the ebullient Randolph Churchill; both are seen here with their wives.

Much has been written about J.J. Astor and Michael Foot, but comparatively little about Lucy Middleton. Yet she carved her own rightful niche in the city's life and contributed to its well-being significantly.

Mrs Delia Osborne remembered that Mrs Middleton worked very hard while she was M.P. from 1945 to 1951. It was she who persuaded the Labour Party to set up a special committee to represent the blitzed areas and she was appointed its vice-chairman. During the 1950–51 Government she signed the report on Government Information Services and Dockyard expenditure, fighting tenaciously to help secure Devonport's uncertain future.

'Before her time in Parliament Mrs Middleton was active in the peace movement of the 1920s,' wrote Mrs Osborne. 'She also acted as political

Some of Plymouth's former and prospective MP's with their spouses: (from left to right) Jim and Lucy Middleton, J.J. Astor and his wife (on the right), Jill Craigie and husband Michael Foot, Randolph Churchill, and wife.

adviser to the Hindu minorities at sittings of the Round Table Conference. She was director and chairman of War on Want for ten years. In 1977 she edited the Women in the Labour Movement's magazine.

'She was greatly interested in protective legislation for women, in maternity and child welfare. In many ways, she was years ahead of her time in the realm of social engineering.'

Mrs Middleton died in 1983, aged eighty-nine. In a tribute, the then Labour group leader on the city council, Ron King, said he did not expect ever to enjoy the pleasure of working with a better constituency M.P. Her husband, Jim, was general secretary of the Labour Party for a period between the two world wars. Altogether they were a fine couple devoted to advancing the cause of socialism as they interpreted it.

~ *CHILDHOOD GAMES AT HARTLEY RESERVOIR* ~

The grassy banks of Hartley Reservoir sparked off childhood memories among some readers, who used to romp down them with great delight.

Mrs J. Squire used to play at Hartley Park with her sisters, about seventy years ago. She recalled a small tuck shop nearby where they could buy a packet of sweets for a ha'penny. They then enjoyed a picnic on the grass.

Mrs B. Griffiths pointed out that during the 1950s the second house seen on the left was occupied by the General Accident Assurance Corporation, for whom she worked. 'If the photo is of the original wall running along

Hartley Reservoir before the water was covered over.

Tavistock Road, there were steps leading to a small doorway, and this was used many times by a "gentleman of the road".'

I have my own memories of Hartley Park because it was a favoured haunt of my cousin, June, and myself when we were children. We lived nearby and loved tumbling down the park's embankments, with much squealing of pleasure and, sometimes, mud-spattered gaiters.

One experience, however, was anything but happy as far as I was concerned. I was cycling past the reservoir, with its beautifully arched, gushing water fountains, when an elderly man suddenly appeared from behind the hedge. He was clutching a gun and rasped at me, 'Get off your bike or I'll shoot you.'

I thought he meant it and rushed to my waiting and bemused friend, a middle-aged lady called Kitty, who comforted me as best she could. The seat on which this touching scene was enacted is still there and I often think of this incident when I stroll past on my way home.

Today, the water in the reservoir is no longer to be seen. South West Water put a concrete cover over it and then grassed it to help make the water purer. Before this was done, it had been subject to droppings from passing pigeons and seagulls, a spokesman said. He also added that one day the grass is likely to be removed.

Author, aged six, and cousin June (*see text*).

SERVICE WITH MORE THAN A SMILE AT GENONI'S

This photograph was taken in the 1950s. It shows the underground toilets near Derry's Clock, with the Continental Hotel looming on the horizon, but it is Genoni's ever-popular Swiss restaurant that most people remember.

Genoni's Swiss
restaurant in the 1950s.

Genoni's Swiss restaurant in the 1950s.

Mr Jack Smyth recalled the 'magnetism' of Genoni's. It specialised in Swiss bakery products, among many other succulent offerings. He said that it became a favourite rendezvous for professional people who worked in the area and for others who had something in common, such as belonging to a club.

'I think most people who knew it well agree that Genoni's really was very special. The careful service, the quality of its surroundings and the whole atmosphere, which carried a touch of the Bohemian, made it different from any other restaurant in the whole of Plymouth. Somehow, it epitomised the city's pre-war ethos, which was far more "snug", convivial and relaxed than it is today, when the centre's vast tracts of open space have smothered all of that.'

Mr Smyth, a retired optician, pointed out that the nineteenth-century Western Evening Herald offices stood a little further west, but that was in the days of horse-trams and cabs.

THE PEACEFUL OASIS
OF WESTWELL GARDENS

Where was the coolest spot in Plymouth on a hot day? Why, none other than Westwell Gardens, said Mrs Enid Ware, pointing out that it was built over an old cemetery. Donald Chapman also remembered it as 'a really peaceful oasis, a spot where one could have a quick snack lunch, say fish and chips and a couple of cakes or doughnuts for the equivalent of three new pence!'

Another reader, known only as 'Stan', identified several of the buildings in the photograph, including, from left to right, George Street Baptist Church,

the Royal Hotel, the Lockyer and Lloyds Bank. He recalled that the church was built of very large granite pieces 'and looked very sombre'.

Part of Westwell Gardens, a haven of quiet on a hot day.

It was anything but sombre inside, however. Ronald Fox remembered its 'star' preacher of the pre-war days, the 'redoubtable and persuasive J. Wilkinson Riddle, who made his mark in several spheres of the city's life, not just the religious. Sometimes you had to queue up a good hour before the evening service began to get a seat, but it was well worth it. His fiery, compelling biblical expositions held that vast congregation without difficulty at all and you left the service really having received something spiritually substantial and nourishing.'

Another building identified by Stan was Shobrooks' auction rooms, nearer the camera and also on the right. This was 'where my father bought me a second-hand girls' bike – to learn on! – which cost the equivalent of 37p'.

It is interesting to note that the remains in the cemetery were removed by night when post-war reconstruction demanded this. Apparently, the city council was worried that local people would be upset if they saw them being carted away in broad daylight.

~ PLYMOUTH ~
MORE PICTURES FROM THE PAST

The following selection of photographs are included to stir up more memories of the city as she was in bygone days.

The Torpoint ferries in 1890, from the Cornish side of the river.

Tavistock Road complete with Hamsom cab and horse-drawn tram, about 1895.

Public School, Coburg Street, 1888.

The old East Street market gate.

Camel's Head, Keyham.

The Hoe from
Grand Hotel.

~ INDEX ~